Group Dating!
■ 301 Ideas ■

Compiled by
Blair & Tristan Tolman

For our party group:
Thanks for trying out
so many ideas with us,
and thanks for the memories!

Coypright © 1999 Blair & Tristan Tolman
All Rights Reserved.

No part of this publication may be reproduced in any form or by any means without permission in writing from the publisher.

Cover photograph by Kelli Weaver, Mauch Portrait Studio

Printed in the United States of America

Contents

Introduction 1

Chapter One:
Physical Group Dates 3

Chapter Two:
Thinking Group Dates 37

Chapter Three:
Group Dates On Location 55

Chapter Four:
Group Dates Involving Water 82

Chapter Five:
Group Dates Around A Table 92

Index 104

Contributors

Susan Adkins
Brad Bateman
Andrew Brandt
Erica Brandt
Sean Buddecke
Darrin Case
Brian and Liberty Cheney
Brad Cowgill
Paul Crozier
Rebecca Gifford
Brad Hart
Jessica Jacobson
Joseph Jenkins
Jerry and Cindy Jensen
Jared Jones
Chris Klaich
Philip Kondrat
Miles Langley
Michael LeBaron
Jeff Martin
Alan and Linda Martineau
Dean Martineau
Karl Martineau

Tamra Martineau
Bill and Kathie Martsolf
Sarah Martsolf
Len and Karen Mendenhall
Ayme Naccarato
Warren Newcombe
Tyler Pearson
John Perotti
Melissa Puddicombe
Bruce and Mari Shawcroft
Joe Shawcroft
Katie Rose Shawcroft
Jim Shortridge
Veldon and Diane Sorenson
Brett and Raelynn Stewart
George and Penni Stoll
Kip Thygerson
Vivien Wade
Rachel Waterhouse
Adam Watkins
Angela Waugh
Jacob White

Introduction

What is group dating? Group dating occurs when two or more couples—or a group of friends—come together in a dating situation. A group date can include a double date, a date of three or more couples, a party where couples are invited, or a party in which friends come without being paired up. In other words, a group date can be about any combination of more than two people of the opposite gender who come together in a social setting.

Why is group dating important? Group dating provides physical safety, spiritual safety, less social stress, and oftentimes more fun. It also helps teenagers develop social skills, make friends, and maintain high moral standards. In the pamphlet *For the Strength of Youth,* the First Presidency of the Church of Jesus Christ of Latter-day Saints counsels youth, "When you begin dating, go in groups or on double dates. Avoid pairing off exclusively with one partner." (p.7) Additionally, since we have been married, we have found that group dating can be as fun for adults as it is for teenagers. Some of our favorite times are at "Party Night," where we and several other married couples get together for a monthly group date together.

Why this book? Knowing the value and the fun of group dating in our own lives and in the lives of the youth with whom we associate, we have collected and compiled hundreds of ideas for fun group dates from many creative young people and adults in order to share them with others. Some of the ideas included in this book can fill a whole evening by themselves, while others are shorter in duration in order to be more suitable for parties where several different activities during the course of the evening are more fun. Our hope is that this book will encourage both teenagers and adults to plan and participate in wholesome, fun, and safe group dating experiences that they will cherish throughout their lives. Have fun!

CHAPTER ONE

Physical Group Dates

Artillery

Play this dodge ball type game on a basketball court. Divide into two teams and give each team two balls and a one-gallon can. Set each can on the ground underneath a basketball hoop, and assign a guard from each team to protect this target. Players try to make a basket in the opposite team's hoop with a ball or knock over the opposite team's can. If a player gets hit with a ball by a member of the other team, he is out of the game, but if someone on his team makes a basket in the opposite team's hoop, everyone from that team who was out of the game is in again. If a player catches the other team's thrown ball, one person who was out from his team comes back in. If a player knocks over the opposing team's can, his team automatically wins.

Backwards Track Meet

With couples as teams, compete against the other couples in track and field events with the rule that all events must be completed backwards. Some events you might try are: the fifty yard dash, the long jump, the very low hurdles, the discus throw (frisbee), the shot put (throw a ball double-handed over your head), and relays with baton passes.

Badminton

Purchase or borrow a badminton set, or make your own using tennis rackets, a volleyball net, and a homemade birdie. (To make a homemade birdie, place a small weight inside of a rag and wrap it in layers of the rag so that it is cushioned. Leave a streamer or tail coming off the end.) Play according to badminton rules if you know them; if not, play using volleyball rules, using the birdie as the volleyball. Use the tennis rackets to serve the birdie and to volley it back and forth.

Balloon Basketball

Play half court basketball using balloons instead of a basketball. Each team has two balloons of its color which are in play simultaneously, so that four balloons are always in play. Both teams have possession all the time. No holding of a balloon is allowed; the balloons must be constantly batted between teammates who are attempting to make a basket. Defensive action consists of batting the other team's balloon to the ground, upon which they must take it out of bounds and bring it in again while the other balloons remain in play. Have extra balloons available in case they pop.

Balloon Bounce

Players lay shoulder to shoulder on their backs in a circle with their feet inward and their heads outward. Fill a large balloon with air, and give it to one player to start the game. She serves the balloon upward into the air above the circle by hitting it with her hand. As it floats downward, someone else must bump the balloon back into the air using his hands or feet. See how many times your group can bump the balloon into the air without it ever touching the ground. No one can move out of the circle.

> **Variation:** Arrange yourselves guy/girl and play guys versus girls. Whichever gender knocks the balloon out of play or lets it land on themselves loses a point.

Bicycle Tag

This activity requires each participant to bring a bicycle. Ride your bikes to a nearby park or other suitable cycling location. Give each person a strip of cloth to tie around his or her arm. Each couple should have matching cloth strips to identify them as a paired team. Give each team a few tennis balls or other soft balls. When ready, allow everyone a few minutes to ride somewhere in the park where they are away from the others. To start, blow a whistle. At the whistle, players attempt to tag the others by getting close enough to hit an enemy's bicycle with a ball. The ball must hit either the rider's bike or her leg, but if it hits her above her waist, the thrower is eliminated from that round. When a person is hit, she is out for that round. The last team with a cyclist untagged wins the round.

> **Variation:** This activity can also be done on foot or on roller blades and can be done in teams of more than one couple each.

Big Game Hunting

For this "safari" at home, hide animal crackers around

the house and announce that your group is going on a big game hunt. Each couple is a team, and teams must hunt around the house for "big game" (animal crackers). Give a time limit, such as ten minutes. The couple with the most crackers at the end of the hunt wins, so don't eat yours until they have been counted!

Body Bumping

For this game, each person must hold his left ankle in his left hand, balance on one foot, and at the "Go" signal, try to hop around and bump the other players off balance. The last person still holding his left foot in his left hand while balancing on his right foot wins.

Bopper

This is a good game to play on a group date with people who don't know each other very well. Begin by choosing someone to be "it." The "it" holds a rolled up newspaper and calls out someone's name in the group and tries to bop her with the newspaper before she calls out someone else's name. If he bops her in time, then he gives her the newspaper and she becomes "it." If he doesn't bop her before she calls out someone else's name, then he must try to bop the person that she named before that person calls out someone else's name.

British Bulldog

Divide the group into two teams. Each team lines up along one side of a playing field. A guy and a girl are chosen to be the bulldogs. The bulldogs go to the center of the field in between the two teams. When the bulldogs yell, "British Bulldog!" the two teams attempt to run to the opposite end of the playing field. Each bulldog tries to catch someone and lift him or her off the ground. When a person is lifted off the ground, he becomes a bulldog. Bulldogs should team up to catch the fastest players. Play until everyone is a bulldog. Hint: Players may want to remove their watches and other jewelry before beginning this game.

Club And Bandanna War

For this date, you will need PVC pipe and water noodles to make several soft clubs. (Water noodles are the long, spaghetti noodle-shaped spongy foam floaters that children often play with in swimming pools.) Cut the pipe into lengths of two, three, or four feet, depending how long you want the clubs to be. Cut the water noodles into lengths which measure 6-10 inches shorter than each length of pipe. Slip the water noodles over the pipes (the extra 6-10 inches of pipe will serve as a handle) and tighten the water noodles onto the pipes by tying them down with strips of rags or twine.

To play, divide into teams. Each player tucks an end of a bandanna into the top of his pants above one of his hips, leaving most of the bandanna exposed. Teams go to opposite ends of a playing field. At the "Go" signal, the two teams approach each other with the goal of trying to remove an enemy's bandanna. They use their clubs to attack the enemy and defend themselves. Players may not strike each other too hard, or on the head, with the clubs. When a player's bandanna is removed, she is out of the game. The last team to have players still in the game wins the round.

Variation: Use your clubs and bandannas to play a strategic game such as Capture The Flag, Capture The King, or Conquer The Castle.

Crab Soccer

Divide into two teams and designate goals and a goalie for each team. All players get in crab position (touching only palms of hands and bottoms of feet to the floor, with torso and head facing upward). Place a soccer ball in the middle of the field.

At the "Go" signal, play soccer while in crab position. Players may rest by sitting down on the ground, but they cannot engage in play unless they are in the crab position. To play this game in an indoor gym, place a piece of masking tape on the end walls about five feet high. To score, a player must kick the soccer ball into the opposing team's wall below the tape.

Croquet

Buy or borrow a croquet set, and set up the game on the lawn. Remember, the shorter the grass is, the further the ball will roll when hit, so mow the lawn before playing. Play as individuals, each with your own ball, or play as couples, taking turns hitting your ball.

> **Variation:** Let the lawn grow tall and then, with a lawn mower, mow ball paths onto the lawn on which the hoops and spikes are placed. A poorly hit ball will end up in the tall grass.

> **Variation:** Play moonlight croquet. Turn your croquet set into a night croquet set by adding stripes of glow-in-the-dark paint to the balls, wires, and posts. Then, play croquet in the light of the moon.

Date Drawing

Get several pieces of banner paper and some crayons,

colored pencils, finger paints, or water colors with which to draw. To begin, pin two large pieces of banner paper to a wall. Blindfold a couple and have them both approach the banner paper. They simultaneously draw each other while blindfolded. The rest of the group gets to watch them draw. Take turns until every couple has drawn each other.

Ding-A-Ling Tag

Select someone to be the "ding-a-ling." Tie a bell around the ankle of the ding-a-ling and blindfold everyone else. At the signal, the blindfolded people scatter to the edges of the room. Then, the ding-a-ling moves around. When the blindfolded people hear the bell of the ding-a-ling, they move towards the ding-a-ling, attempting to catch her. The ding-a-ling's task is to evade the blindfolded players for as long as possible. Whoever catches the ding-a-ling first chooses the next ding-a-ling.

Dinner Darts

Ask each couple to bring a specific finger food to this group date such as baby carrots, crackers, cheese squares, baby pickles, olives, donuts, eclairs, or pizza rounds. Arrange these foods on a table in a circular fashion, resembling a circular dart board. Place the most desirable foods towards the center of the circle. Then play darts with a real dart board and darts. After each throw, a player gets to eat one serving of the type of food that corresponds with the circle he hit on the dartboard. Play until the food is gone or until everyone is full.

Down By The Banks

For this activity, everyone sits in a circle, legs crossed (Indian style), facing inward. Each person places his hands on his knees, palms up. His right hand sits on top of the left hand of the person sitting to his right, and his left hand sits under the right hand of the person sitting to his left. Pick someone to start the game. To start, the group begins to sing the song, *Down By The Banks*. (One version of this song goes, "Down by the banks of the hanky panky where the bullfrogs jump from bank to banky, with an eeeps! Iiips! Ooops! Aups! You missed the lilly pad and went kerplop!")

While you sing the song, the first person lifts his right hand, reaches over, and slaps the right hand of the person to his left. The person to his left then lifts her right hand, reaches over, and slaps the right hand of the person to her left. Continue around the circle in this pattern until the end of the song, which ends with the word, "Kerplop." The person whose hand is slapped on the word "Kerplop" is out for that round and has to leave the circle. Play continues until there is only one person left, and he is declared the winner.

Drawing Relay

Divide into two teams. Each team needs a few sheets of paper, a pencil, and a table. The tables should be 5-10 feet apart from each other. Select someone to be the referee. The referee stands in between the tables and holds a list of words to be drawn. A player from each team approaches the referee, who shows them the first word on his list. The players run to their tables and draw the word on a piece of paper for their groups, using only pictures (no letters or numbers). As soon as one team member guesses the word correctly, the next person on that team runs to the referee and gets a new word, which she draws for her team. The other team must continue guessing the first word until someone guesses it correctly, and then another member of that team may get the second word from the referee. The person drawing the picture cannot say anything; he can only nod or shake his head. The first group to successfully draw and guess every word on the referee's list wins. Hint: Players should whisper their guesses so the other team won't overhear the correct word as it is guessed.

Dress Up Relay

Fill two large boxes with equal amounts of gloves, hats, socks, shoes, scarves, coats, sunglasses, and other accessories. Make several different lists of the items in each box, each list having the same items but in a different order. Divide your group into two teams and give each team one of the lists. Blindfold the first person on each team.

On the "Go" signal, each blindfolded person approaches her box and her teammates look at their list and yell out the first item she is to locate and put on while she is blindfolded. After she has put that item on, her teammates tell her the second item to put on, and so forth, until she is wearing every item from her box. The blindfolded opponents race to get the items on, one by one. When one player finishes putting on all of the items on the list, she removes her blindfold and the items from the box and puts the items back in the box. She rushes her blindfold to the next person on her team.

The next person blindfolds himself and approaches the box while his team gets a new list to use for this round. His teammates tell him the order to put on the items, as before. Continue playing, racing the other team, until everyone on one team has had a turn wearing the blindfold and putting on all of the accessories. The fastest team wins.

Variation: Place all of the clothes in a pile in the middle of the floor and let the opponents race for the items blindfolded, as their teammates call the items out to them in order.

Easter Egg Color Tag

Scatter several plastic Easter eggs outside in a yard or field. Someone is "it" and he calls out the name of a color. Everyone must run to an Easter egg of that color and touch it before he gets tagged by the person who is "it." If a player touches an Easter egg before he gets tagged, he is safe, but if he gets tagged first, he is "it" for the next round.

Egg Toss

For this activity, each couple needs at least a dozen raw eggs. Go to a field and line up with guys in one line and girls in another line facing the guys, with couples across from each other. The lines should be about five feet apart. Everyone should have access to several eggs each. On the count of three, the girls simultaneously toss one of their eggs to their dates. The dates must catch the eggs without cracking or breaking them. If an egg cracks or breaks, the couple is out. After the first throw, all the remaining couples must then take one giant step backwards and on the count of three, the guys toss one egg to their dates, playing as before. Continue in this fashion until only one couple remains in the game. That couple wins. Play as many times as you have eggs to use.

Variation: Turn this egg toss into Egg Roulette by boiling half of the eggs before playing. Leave all eggs unmarked so you can't tell which eggs are boiled and which ones are raw . . . that is, until they crack.

PHYSICAL GROUP DATES 13

Fast Blast

For this game, one person lays on the floor under a blanket with his hands at his sides. Everyone else stands one step away from him with their hands behind their backs, forming a circle around the person under the blanket. One person standing in the circle holds a rolled up newspaper behind her back. With the newspaper, she bops the guy laying under the blanket and then quickly hides the newspaper behind her back. Upon being bopped, the guy under the blanket flings the blanket off his face and attempts to identify the person who hit him. If he identifies her correctly, she replaces the guy under the blanket and the game begins again. If he can't identify her correctly, he goes under the blanket again for another round.

Feather Volleyball

Locate a small, light feather that floats easily in the air. To play, simply tie a string between two pieces of furniture as the volleyball net. Also, designate which areas are out of bounds. Give each player a breath mint, and then play feather volleyball by blowing the feather back and forth across the net. There are no limits as to how many blows it takes to get the feather over the net, but if a team lets the feather touch the ground, the other team scores a point. If you desire, you can play this game on your hands and knees, depending on how high you put the net.

Feeding Frenzy

Blindfold all participants, and then give each couple a different type of food (such as cookies, licorice, or marshmallows.) Couples should not know what food the others have been given or where their dates are. Spin everyone around, and then instruct them to find and feed their dates.

A player finds his date by first tasting what is in his own hand, and then finding someone else and putting a bite of the food into her mouth. If she has the same type of food in her hand, it means she is his date and will indicate it to him by accepting another bite of food. If she will not accept another bite of food from him, it means she is not his date, and he must continue his search.

When a couple finds each other, they quickly feed each other all of the food in their hands and then yell that they are finished. This couple wins. No noises or touching of faces is allowed during the search as this would help identify people, and for sanitation purposes, use only small, single-bite foods for this activity.

Flag Football

Meet at a park or playing field and set up boundaries and two touchdown zones for the football field. Divide into two teams. Provide each player with two flags (strips of cloth, one color per team) which they tuck into their pants at the hip so that everyone is wearing a flag on each hip. To play, follow basic football rules but instead of tackling an opponent, you must remove one of his flags.

Flour War

To prepare several flour ball bombs for this date, cut old nylons into squares and then put about 1/4 cup of flour into each square. Tie the ends of the nylon together, creating a ball of flour entrapped inside the nylon. When a player throws the flour ball and hits someone, the nylon stretches on impact, allowing some of the flour to sift through the nylon and leave a flour mark on the person hit.

To play, divide into two teams and divide the flour bombs amongst the players. At the "Go" signal, players attack each other with flour bombs by throwing the bombs at each other (no head shots). When a person is hit, he is out of the game for three minutes. Play continues until one team wins by marking all members of the opposing team with flour.

> **Variation:** Use your flour bombs to play a strategic game such as Capture The Flag, Capture The King, or Conquer The Castle.

German Spotlight

Play this game in the dark. Select one couple to be the "seekers" and the other couples to be the "hiders." Couples must stay in pairs for the entire duration of this game. (Tie his hand to her hand, if you have to!) The seekers carry a flashlight and use it to find the other couples who are hiding somewhere in the designated playing area. A couple is caught when the seekers identify them using the beam of the flashlight. The first couple caught will be "it" for the next round, but play continues until all couples are found and identified.

> **Variation:** Play Kick The Can in the dark. Use the same rules as German Spotlight but set a tin can at home base which the seekers must jump over after identifying a hiding couple. Hiding couples can become "free" by kicking the can while the seekers are searching for them.

Glow-Stick Tag

On a dark night, find an open grassy area in which to play Glow-Stick Tag. To play, each participant needs a glow-stick (a plastic tube with chemicals inside which light up and glow when the tube is bent in half until a popping sound is heard and the glowing chemicals are released). Each player should strap his glow-stick to a part of his body where it can be readily seen. Play tag in the dark.

Variation: Have members of each team tie their glow-sticks to the same parts of their bodies (for example, Team A members tie their sticks to their hips while Team B members tie their sticks to their ankles) and play tag in teams.

Halloween Bowling

Purchase at least one small, round pumpkin for each person (the more round the better). For a Halloween night activity, set up a bowling alley on a hard surface. Use empty two-liter plastic soda pop bottles for the bowling pins and use the pumpkins for the bowling balls. Keep score as in bowling and play with couples as teams.

Heads-N-Hands

Stand as a group in a large circle. Blindfold one person and place him in the middle of the circle. When he claps, everyone changes places and forms a new circle. The blindfolded person moves toward one person in the circle and, after finding one, feels only her head or hands and then tries to identify her. If he identifies her correctly, she is in the middle. If not, he tries to identify someone else.

Hit-N-Run

Everyone in the group sits in a large circle, facing inward. Select someone to stand in the middle of the circle next to a box containing a "club" (an old sock stuffed with paper or rags). To play, she takes the club out of the box and hits one of the people in the circle on the knee and then quickly races back to the middle of the circle and puts the club back in the box. The person she hit immediately rises and tries to retrieve the club from the box and hit her back before she steals his vacant seat in the circle. If he hits her back before she sits in his seat, she is in the middle for the next round. If she sits in his seat before he can retrieve the club and hit her, then he is in the middle for the next round.

Hoop Dodge Ball

In an indoor gym, use the half-court line of the basketball court to create two equal sides of play. Place four volleyballs on the half-court line. Divide the group into two teams and instruct all players of both teams to touch the wall on their side of the court with one of their feet.

At the "Go" signal, players race towards the volleyballs and try to get them. The players that get a ball throw them at players of the opposite team to try to hit their legs with the balls. If a player gets hit with a ball, he is out of the game. If a player hits another player above the waist, he is out of the game. Once a ball has been thrown, another player can pick it up and throw it towards somebody else. At any time, a person from either team may risk crossing the dividing line into the opposing team's territory and attempt to shoot the volleyball through the basketball hoop. If he succeeds in making a basket without getting hit by a ball first, all players from his team who are out come back into the game.

Human Air Hockey

Divide into two teams and select a large, smooth floor to be the playing area. Mark a goal on each side of the playing area which players must defend. Players position themselves on their side of the playing area. To begin play, drop a ping pong ball in the center of the playing area. Teams attempt to blow the ping pong ball into the other team's goal. No goalies are allowed, and the ball can never touch a person's body. If the ball comes towards someone, she must move to give it free passage. If the ball touches a player, the other team scores a point. A team scores a point whenever it blows the ball into the other team's goal. Then remove the ball from the goal, drop it into the center of the playing area, and begin again. The team with the most points wins.

Human Foosball

This date works best with 14 or more people. Go to a park or other large playing area and give each participant a 10 foot length of PVC pipe. Divide into two teams and tie blue strips of cloth around the arms of one team, and red strips of cloth around the arms of the other. Set up a goal on each end of the playing field, one for each team.

Position the players as in table Foosball, with a row of three people from one team in front of its goal, holding their pipes at arm's length, approximately 25 feet apart from each other. About 25 feet down the field, position a row of players of the opposite team. Continue positioning rows of players down the field, alternating teams, until all players have been assigned a place. During the game, players cannot move from where they are standing, but can only swing their pipes to move the ball.

A player in the middle of the playing field hits a volleyball with his pipe towards the opposite goal. As the ball passes through a participant's playing circle, she tries to move it towards the other team's goal, as in table Foosball. A team scores one point every time the ball rolls into the other team's goal. The team that scores the most points wins.

Human Pinwheel

All participants remove their shoes. Select one person to be the pinwheel. She puts both feet together, stands as straight and stiff as possible, and places her arms across her chest. Everyone else sits in a tight circle around her, pressing their feet up against her ankles. Her feet are now anchored to the floor by everyone else's. She then leans and begins falling in any direction. The people in the circle put their arms up, catch her, and bounce her to the left, the right, or straight across the circle. Continue until the circle breaks or until she bends and collapses into the circle. Choose someone else to be in the middle and continue as before.

Human Tug-O-War

Divide into two teams. Each team's players line up one behind the other, with each team facing the other. Teammates should link up to each other by placing their hands around the waist of the person in front of them. The front person on each team holds the wrists of the person of the other team facing him. Mark a horizontal line on the floor in between the front player of each team. At the "Go" signal, both teams begin pulling backwards. The first team to pull three opposing team members across the line wins. Remember: Your chain is only as strong as its weakest link, so be prepared for a backward fall if it breaks.

Human Tunnel Race

Divide into two or more teams. Select a starting line and designate a finish line several yards away from the starting line. Players line up as teams, one behind the other at the starting line. At the "Go" signal, the first person on each team stands on the starting line and spreads his legs apart, forming a tunnel. The second player on each team crawls through the opened legs of her teammate and stands up an arm's length in front of him. He places his hands on her waist and she also forms a tunnel with her legs. The tunnel is now two people deep. A third player then crawls through the tunnel and links on in front in similar fashion, and the chain continues.

After the last player on the team has crawled through the tunnel, the person who started it then crawls through, and the tunnel advances with the person in back always breaking off and crawling through the tunnel to the front. Each team's human tunnel slowly advances in this fashion towards the finish line. The first team to have every member across the finish line wins.

Hunter And Hounds

Divide into teams and assign each team a leader. The leader in each group is the hunter and the others in the group are the hounds. Obtain several handfuls of colored jelly beans (one color per team) and hide them throughout the playing area. Make sure there is an equal number of beans for each team. Tell each group which color bean it is supposed to hunt.

At the "Go" signal, the hounds in each group begin looking for their beans. While searching for them, they cannot make any noise or move any objects. When a hound spots a bean of his team's color, he remains near the bean and howls like a hound until his team's hunter comes to him. The hunter must find the bean and pick it up. In the process, the hound can only look at the bean and point with facial gestures. The winning team is the first to collect all its beans.

Karaoke
Rent or borrow a Karaoke machine and have a singing night with your group. Take turns singing to all kinds of different songs. Sing solos, duets, or group songs. Videotape the performance for future laughs.

Kissing Rugby
Assign each guy in your group a number and each girl in your group a letter of the alphabet. In a large room, position the guys on one side of the room and the girls on the other side. A guy in the middle of the room calls out both a letter and a number. The girl with that letter rushes to kiss the guy in the middle of the room on the cheek while the guy with that number rushes to kiss the girl on the cheek before she reaches the guy in the middle. Whoever loses goes in the middle for the next round. Occasionally during the game, let players switch their letters or numbers.

> **Variation:** Sit in a large circle where the guys and girls are mixed instead of on opposite sides.

Kneepad Olympics
Couples wear kneepads and compete in Kneepad Olympics by competing in Olympic events while on their knees. Some events to include:

> 1) Tandem Race: Each couple links together by tying his right shoelace to her left shoelace, then kneeling side by side. He connects his right hand to her left hand

with a large, thick rubber band. Race on knees to a certain point and back.

2) Hurdles: Place a yardstick on bricks to create a hurdle. Position several hurdles between the starting line and the finish line. Racers run on their knees towards the finish line, and are penalized three seconds for every yardstick they knock off on their way.

3) Long Jump: Kneel at a starting line and swing your arms forward to gain momentum to jump forward as far as possible. Mark the spot of furthest advancement for each person and measure the distance.

Lawn Tag

Mow a maze of lines on your lawn and use it for a playing area. Play tag on the lawn, requiring that players remain on the maze of mowed grass for the entire game. One person is chosen to be "it" and she gives the other players ten seconds to scatter throughout the mowed maze. Then she races after them. When she catches someone, he becomes the new "it."

Limbo

Everybody limbo! Turn on some music that has a good beat and use a broomstick or yardstick for a limbo stick. A couple holds the stick horizontally at shoulder length and everyone else forms a line, one couple behind another, facing the limbo stick. Couples hold hands while they attempt to pass under the stick simultaneously without bending forward from the waist up. After everyone has attempted passing under the stick at the first height, the people holding the stick lower it an inch or two and everyone attempts to pass under it at the second height. Continue passing under the stick, which gets gradually lower towards the ground with each round. If someone touches the stick or falls to the ground, that couple is out of the game. The game ends when only one couple is left "limboing." This couple wins.

Mop Hockey

Play this game either in an indoor gym or in some other wide open area with a smooth floor. Get one mop for every person that will be playing. The mops need to have rectangular sponge heads. You can use them as they are, but they sometimes slide along the floor better if they are first wrapped in duct tape. To play, set up goals on each end of the room and divide into teams. Use a tennis ball for the puck and the mops for the hockey sticks. Follow normal hockey rules and include the rule that no one can lift his mop head off the floor at any time. (This will prevent high sticking and injuries.)

Musical Chairs

Set up a ring of chairs facing outward with one less chair than there are participants. Play some music from the radio, cassette, or compact disc. While the music is playing, all participants walk in a circle around the outside of the chairs. When the music stops, participants must sit down in a chair as quickly as possible. The person left without a chair is out, and another chair is removed from the circle. Continue playing until only one winner remains.

> **Variation:** Play Musical Chairs by using the guys as the chairs. The guys each kneel on one knee with the other remaining horizontally as a chair. When the music stops, each girl must find a knee and sit on it.

The girl left standing is out, and a guy is removed as well for the following round.

One Shot

For this game, each player needs something to roll, toss, bounce, or slide. Pick an object to be your target. Each player tosses, rolls, bounces, or slides his object towards the target. Whoever gets his object closest to the target without touching it wins that round.

Picture Mania

Divide the group into teams and let each team select a captain. Each team should have a chalkboard and some chalk. Give each team captain an identical set of cards, such as:

Card #1 = RABBIT: ears, tail, nose, feet, body, eyes, mouth, whiskers

Card #2 = HOUSE: door, walkway, window, walls, chimney, roof, garage

Card #3 = SCHOOL BUS: windows, kids, driver, wheels, door, exhaust

At the "Go" signal, each team captain calls out the first descriptive word on his first card ("ears"). The first person on his team runs to that team's chalkboard and draws a set of ears, without knowing they are supposed to be rabbit ears. The captain then calls out the second word ("tail") and the second player runs to the chalkboard and adds his object to the picture. Continue in this fashion, drawing the words on the first card in order until a team figures out what the object is supposed to be and calls it out. This team gets a point. Play additional rounds with additional cards for as long as you desire. The team with the most points at the end of the game wins.

> **Variation:** Play the same as above, but the team captains tell their teams what the object is before anyone begins to draw it. The team that finishes drawing the object first (recognizably), using every descriptive word on the card, scores a point.

Pine Cone Toss

This is a fun activity to play while you are on a picnic in the mountains, but it can be played in nearly any outdoor area. Set up a pine cone toss by making a 5" x 5" square in the dirt, and then dividing it into four smaller squares by making a plus sign through the middle of it. Using a stick, carve a number 5 into the soil of the lower left square. Carve a number 10 in the lower right square, a number 15 in the upper right square, and a number 20 in the upper left square. About 25 feet away from the square, draw a starting line in the soil. The group stands on the starting line and takes turns tossing pine cones towards the square. Every time your pine cone lands in a numbered square, you score that number of points. Play singly or with couples as teams.

> **Variation:** For an indoor variation to this group date, have a bean bag toss instead. Mark off your squares and numbers on a carpeted area of a large room with masking tape. Play singly or with couples as teams.

Potato Bowling

Make a large circular target on a sidewalk or driveway using sidewalk chalk. Include points on the target, with the highest number of points on the bull's eye in the center of the target. From a starting line several feet away, roll potatoes down the sidewalk onto the target. If a potato lands on a numbered section of the target, that couple scores that many points. Keep score and give a prize to the winning couple.

Pumpkin Piñata Party

Hollow out pumpkins and fill them with individually-wrapped candies, creating pumpkin piñatas. Paint funny or scary faces on the pumpkins with craft paints and let them dry. The piñatas will be moist and heavy, so be sure to hang them outside with sturdy twine or rope. Take turns blindfolding each other and trying to hit a piñata with a stick. When a piñata breaks, race to gather the candy.

Purse And Wallet Scavenger Hunt

For this scavenger hunt, write down a bunch of items that might be found in either a purse or a wallet. Couples play as teams. To begin, the host calls out an item. Couples scramble to find the item and race it to the host. The fastest couple to present the host with the correct item wins a point. Play by calling out a variety of items for as long as you desire. At the end of the game, the couple with the most points wins.

Red Flag Blue Flag

Each person ties a red and blue bandanna together and the group divides into two teams. Tuck the flags into the back pockets of each player, with the blue bandanna hanging out if that person is on the blue team and the red bandanna hanging out if that person is on the red team. Everyone sneaks around in the bushes of an outdoor playing area, trying to capture each other's flag. When a person captures the flag of a player on the other team, he gives it back to that player who must reverse the color and join the other team, so that he is now hunting members of his previous color. The game is over when everyone is on the same color team.

Red Rover

Divide into two equal teams and line up across a playing field facing the opposite team. Players stand side by side holding hands, far enough apart from each other that their hands are stretched taut. The first team selects a person from the opposite team and chants, "Red Rover, Red Rover, send (name of person) right over!" That person must run as fast as she can right into the linked hands of two people on her opposing team and try to break through their hands. If she does, she is free to return to her own team, taking someone from this team back to her own. If she doesn't, she must stay as a new member of her opposing team and link hands with two people in that line. The game continues until one entire team has been eliminated.

Scatter

Obtain a soft ball such as a volleyball or a foam ball. One person throws the ball against a wall and it bounces back towards the crowd. The participants either run from the ball or run towards it, trying to pick it up. The person that picks up the ball scores a point. Once someone picks up the ball, everyone must freeze. Then, each person can take three steps in any direction and stop. The person with the ball throws it at someone and tries to hit her legs with it. If he hits someone, he scores another point. However, if the targeted person catches the ball before it hits her legs, she scores a point. Play as many rounds as you desire. The person with the most points within a given time period wins.

Sneaky Sneak

Sneaky Sneak is a nocturnal outdoor game in which one couple hides an object (such as a handkerchief) in the trees and at the "Go" signal, the rest of the couples try to find it. Each couple should have and use a flashlight. The couple to find the object scores a point and gets to hide the object for the next round.

Snow Buffalo

Go with your group to a large, snow-covered field and divide into two buffalo herds. Select a guy and a girl to stand in between the two herds of buffalo. These two are wolves.

To play, the wolves yell, "Buffalo!" At this cue, the two herds of buffalo stampede through the snow towards each other and the awaiting wolves, with the goal of safely reaching the opposite side of the field. In the midst of the stampede, the wolves attempt to catch a buffalo and lift him or her off the ground. Once a buffalo has been caught and lifted off the ground, he or she becomes a wolf for the next stampede. Play continues in stampedes until no buffalo are left.

Snow Fort Wars

On a winter day when the snow is good for packing, get some couples together to make snow forts and have a snow fort war. Each couple should make its own fort. To make a fort out of snow bricks, pack some snow into a rectangular plastic container and then slide out a nice snow brick. Stack the bricks on top of each other to make a snow fort. After everyone's fort is built, make snowballs and attack each other's forts with them.

Snow Volleyball

Stomp out boundary lines in the snow, set up a volleyball net, wear warm clothing, and play volleyball in the snow.

Snowshoe Olympics

Host the Snowshoe Olympics. Members of your group are the Olympic athletes. Some Olympic events you could include are: the standing long jump, the running long jump, the high jump (over a piece of yarn), the fifty yard dash, the hurdles, the 100-yard relay (by passing a baton to another athlete every 25 yards), and the shot-put.

Snowshoes can be purchased, rented, or made. One way to make snowshoes is with the lids of five-gallon plastic buckets, one lid per foot. Center one boot on one lid, and then cut one-inch slits through the lid near each side of the boot. Insert a piece of surgical tubing into each slit and then tie a knot in the tubing beneath the lid. Slide your boot beneath the surgical tube strap.

Snowshoe Softball

Everyone must wear snowshoes to play Snowshoe Softball. Use a large rubber ball or old volleyball instead of a softball so that the ball won't get lost in the snow. Players can wear winter gloves instead of mitts. Softball rules apply. Snowshoes can be purchased, rented, or made. For instructions on how to make homemade snowshoes, see "Snowshoe Olympics" above.

Stealth

Divide into two teams. Members of one team wear blindfolds and hats and carry rolled up newspapers. Members of the other team attempt to remove the hats from the opposing team's heads without getting swatted with the rolled up newspapers. If one player successfully removes a hat, he gets to wear the hat, take the newspaper, and switch teams with the de-hatted player. The goal is to get and remain on the blindfolded team for as long as possible.

Stretch

Place a large paper grocery bag, opened up, on the middle of the floor with participants standing around it. The first person bends down and, placing her lips or teeth on the edge of the bag, grabs the bag in her mouth and stands up, lifting the bag off the floor. She then tears off the soiled portion of the bag and play moves to the person to her left. While attempting to get the bag, no part of a player's body can touch the floor except for her feet. If a person touches the floor during the attempt to pick up the bag, she is out of the game. Gradually, as people grab the bag and tear off portions of it, the bag gets shorter and shorter and the people attempting to pick it up have to stretch further and further. The last person still in the game wins. Make sure everyone stretches out before playing this game.

T-Ball

Play T-Ball together using a child's plastic T-ball set. Rules are the same as for baseball except that the pitcher does not throw the ball to the batter; the batter hits the ball off the T instead.

Tandem Bike Riding

Rent tandem bicycles and enjoy biking around, one couple per bicycle. For a little competition, select a large, vacant parking lot and set up an obstacle course for the bicycles. Time each other as you race to a finish line, to see which couple bikes the fastest.

Three-Legged Sports Night

Divide your group into couples and have each couple stand side by side while you tie their inside legs together. Then, while the pairs remain tied together, play several sports such as soccer, basketball, volleyball, and softball.

Tickle

For this ticklish activity, participants sit in a circle with one person in the middle of the circle. He gets to hold a feather and has ten seconds to use the feather to try to make someone laugh. He cannot touch the victim with anything but the feather. If the victim cracks a smile, flinches, or laughs within ten seconds, she must be in the middle of the circle. If she can keep a solemn face for ten seconds, the tickler approaches someone else and tries again.

Toe Races

Give each couple about ten different objects such as a marble, a pencil, and a penny. Each couple should have the same types of objects. Instruct couples to take their shoes and socks off and stand side by side along a starting line. Place a bucket for each couple at a finish line about 15 feet away from where everyone is standing. Have the couples spread their ten objects out near them at the starting line. At the "Go" signal, players race to pick up their objects using only their toes. After picking up an object, a player must carry it with her toes down to her bucket and deposit the object in the bucket before running back to the starting line for another object. The couple which gets all ten of its objects in its bucket first wins.

Tomato War

Find a farmer or other tomato grower who has overripe, unwanted tomatoes and ask his permission to use his tomatoes in a tomato war. Dress in grubbies. Take your ammunition (the overripe tomatoes) to the playing area (an approved wooded area would work well) and have a tomato war. Protective eye gear is a must, as is a place to wash off when you're done.

Trampoline Add On

To play Trampoline Add On, participants surround a large trampoline and take turns doing tricks. The first person climbs on the trampoline and does a trick, such as bouncing from the knees to the feet. The second person must do the first trick and then without stopping, add on another, such as bounce backwards onto the back and then bounce forward onto the belly. The third person then does the previous two tricks and then adds on a third, and so on. Play advances with people dropping out who are not able to properly perform the sequence of tricks. Obviously, the more experienced jumpers should go last.

Trampoline Catch

This activity tests a couple's hand-eye coordination. One person attempts to throw a soft football to his date who is jumping on a large trampoline. After she catches the ball, she attempts to throw it back to her date. Count their consecutive catches; each is worth a point. When they fail to catch a pass, it's another couple's turn.

Trampoline Crack The Egg

Select someone to be the "egg." This person sits in the middle of the trampoline with his legs crossed, holding his feet with his hands. The others bounce around the edges of the trampoline, attempting to bounce him so that he "cracks," or, lets go of one of his feet. When the egg cracks, select another person to be the egg. To avoid accidents, be careful not to bounce anyone too high.

Tunnel Ball

Divide into two or more teams. Select a starting line and designate a finish line several yards away from the starting line. Players line up as teams, one behind the other at the starting line, with their feet spread apart, forming a tunnel between their legs. They link together with their hands on the hips of the person in front of them.

At the "Go" signal, the person at the front of the tunnel bends down and attempts to roll a soccer ball to the end of the tunnel. The rest of the team helps it along the way by swatting it with their hands. If the ball bounces out of the tunnel, the person at the end of the line retrieves it, returns it to the front person, and runs back to his place at the back of the line. Once the ball reaches the end of the tunnel, the last person picks it up, runs it to the front of the tunnel, and rolls it through. He becomes the new front person. The team continues in this fashion, progressing forward in a race toward the finish line. The first one with the entire team across the finish line is the winner.

Twister With A Twist

Make your own version of a *Twister* game mat by cutting out colored circles of fabric and placing velcro or tape on the backs of them. Randomly place the circles on the floor, in no particular pattern. Play using *Twister* game rules, spinning a dial to call out the movement of feet and hands to colored circles, but using your homemade *Twister* mat. As with the game *Twister,* no two people can share the same circle, so speed in reaching the colored spots is important. As participants twist into pretzel-like positions, they are eliminated either when they touch the floor with any part of their bodies other than their feet or hands, or when they cannot reach the called colored circle.

Ultimate Frisbee

Divide into two teams and line up at opposite ends of a playing field. Set up an end zone for each team. To begin the game, members of team #1 toss the frisbee back and forth between its players towards its end zone, careful to never let it touch the ground. Players should count the number of successful consecutive tosses. If the frisbee hits the ground or is intercepted by a member of team #2, team #2 gets control of the frisbee and counting starts over.

During the time a team has control of the frisbee, members of the other team run down the field and attempt to knock the frisbee to the ground or intercept it. No physical contact between players is allowed. When either team successfully throws the frisbee into its end zone and a member of that same team catches it, this team scores a point for every successful consecutive toss between players during that team's possession.

Unwrap The Present

Everyone comes to this date with a wrapped gift to give away. Stand in a circle and decide who will be person #1. Give him a pair of gloves, a stocking hat, and a present, and give the next person in the circle a pair of dice.

At the "Go" signal, person #1 tries to put on the gloves and hat and then unwrap the present before someone rolls doubles with the dice. While he is trying to unwrap the present, the rest of the people in the circle take turns rolling the dice, in an attempt to roll doubles. As soon as someone rolls doubles, person #1 must take off the gloves and hat and pass them with the present to that person who then puts on the hat and gloves and tries to unwrap the present while the rest of the players continue to try to roll doubles and steal the present.

Continue in this fashion until someone finally unwraps the entire present. The person that finishes unwrapping the present gets to keep it and is out of the game for the next round. Continue playing until everyone has a present to keep.

Walleyball

To play Walleyball, set up a volleyball net in a racquetball court. Play volleyball with the additional rule that the volleyball can be played off the walls and the ceiling. To find a court in which to play, call sports arenas in your area to see which racquetball courts are equipped for Walleyball.

Wolves And Rabbits

Walk into a fresh field of snow and stomp out a circular area about fifteen feet in diameter. This circle is the "rabbit den." Then stomp out a line of about forty feet which leads straight out of the rabbit den. This trail is the "wolf path." Also from the rabbit den, stomp out several crooked trails leading away from the den which curve, loop, and criss-cross through the snow. Some of these trails should lead back to the rabbit den, and some should dead end away from it. Divide your group into rabbits and wolves, with half as many wolves as rabbits.

To play, the rabbits gather in the den and the wolves stand at the far end of the wolf path. At a given signal, the wolves race down the wolf path towards the rabbit den while the rabbits scatter into the maze. The wolves pursue the rabbits through the maze until they have each caught a rabbit. Both wolves and rabbits must stay on the trails at all times. The captured rabbits become wolves for the following round.

> **Variation:** Add a hunter or two to the game. The hunters roam the maze, throwing snowballs at the wolves. A hit wolf must stop in his tracks and count out loud to ten, allowing the rabbits to flee away from him. You could also add a safety pocket on the outer edge of a few of the trails which one rabbit at a time can occupy for one minute each round.

Yarn Maze Race

Before this race, tie a 40-foot piece of colored yarn to a piece of furniture and then wind the yarn through the room going over, under, and around other pieces of furniture. Prepare one such maze of yarn for each couple, letting each piece of yarn criss-cross over the other trails of yarn.

Give each couple the loose end of its piece of yarn. At the "Go" signal, couples race each other to roll their lengths of yarn into a ball all the way to the piece of furniture to which it was originally tied. Hint: To make this game easier, use a different color of yarn for each couple.

CHAPTER TWO

Thinking Group Dates

Backword

Each player needs paper and a pencil to play this game. The first player chooses a 5 or 6 letter word (for example, "flavor"). Each player writes the letters of the word vertically with a line following each letter. They then write the letters of the same word vertically again, but this time from the bottom up next to each line. For example:

```
F _____ r
L _____ o
A _____ v
V _____ a
O _____ l
R _____ f
```

Participants then have three minutes to think of the biggest words they can, using the letters on either side of each line as the first and last letters of each word. (The played upon word cannot be used to fill in a blank, as it would always fit on the first line.) After three minutes, players stop writing and take turns reading each other their words. If any two players have written the same word on the same line number, both players must cross the word off and not count it for points. The rest of a player's words are worth one point per letter. For example, in the game above, a possible word for line #1 is "forever," which would be worth 7 points.

Brown Bags

Put 12 household objects into brown paper lunch bags, one object per bag. Number the bags 1 - 12 on the outside of the bags with a magic marker and seal them with a staple so no one can look inside. Have each person feel the objects through the bags and write down on a piece of paper what he thinks each object is. When everyone has felt each bag, share the answers and give a prize to the person who has correctly identified the most objects. Objects to feel might include: a stapler, scissors, a thimble, a banana, a tube of toothpaste, and a toy car.

> **Variation:** Instead of placing objects in bags to feel and identify, place objects in bags to smell and identify. Participants cannot touch the bags, but can only smell the aroma coming from the top of each bag. Tie the top of each bag partially closed with a string so that players cannot look inside the bag and identify the object inside. Objects to smell might include: cinnamon, vanilla, shoe polish, ammonia, and rose petals.

Categories

Sit in circle and select one person to stand in the middle of the circle. He points to someone in the circle and yells out a category (for example: "shampoo brands" or "vegetables") and then quickly counts to ten out loud. The chosen player must name something in that category (for example: "Finesse" or "carrot") before he counts to ten. If she cannot name something in that category in the given time, then she is in the middle. If she does name something, the person in the middle must point to another person and call out a different category. Hint: Change the count to 5 if 10 seconds seems too easy for your group.

Change Challenge

All participants need some loose change in their pockets to play this game. A person in the group calls out a number under 100, and everyone reaches into his pockets to try to locate the exact change equal to the number called. The change must be located without looking at it, but by feeling it only. When someone thinks she has the right amount, she says, "Got it!" and shows her coins. The first person to have the correct amount wins that round.

> **Variation:** This game can also be played with dates as teams, pooling their coins together to make the correct change. They still cannot look at their coins while counting them, but must feel in their pockets and discuss what they have and what they need from their partners to make the correct amount.

Eagle Eyes

Give each couple a detailed map of the same state. Everyone but the lead couple begins with their maps face down. The starting couple scans its map for ten seconds and chooses a landmark on the map. They announce the landmark to the other couples who must then flip their maps over and scan it together, trying to find it on their maps.

The couple that finds it first scores a point. Take turns being the lead couple.

Extemporaneous Speaking

Develop your abilities to speak in front of a crowd during this group date. Have everyone bring several current national news magazines to the date. Select topics that could serve as subjects for short speeches. During the date, each person should choose a topic that he or she would be willing to prepare a speech about. Give everyone thirty minutes to search through the magazines and obtain information for their speeches. If you desire, you can provide index cards on which they can take notes. Speeches should be five to eight minutes in length. After everyone has finished preparing, take turns giving your speeches to each other.

Fact Or Fiction?

Prior to this date, come up with dozens of facts that are probably not well known but are true. Also come up with several things that sound true, but are actually fictional. Prepare statements from a variety of categories. Since you will know whether each statement is fact or fiction, you and your date will be the moderators for this activity.

Give each couple a statement. They should discuss it and try to determine whether it is fact or fiction, and then announce their decision. They get a point if they are right. Sample questions from the "animal" category:

1) The sex of an alligator is determined by the heat of the nest it was incubated in. (Fact.)
2) Bat droppings are called "guano." (Fact.)
3) When an elephant dies, the other adult elephants from the herd spray dirt on the carcass in a form of

burial. (Fiction.)
4) Killer Whales swim in groups called "pods." (Fact.)
5) An adult male reindeer is called a "stud." (Fiction.)

Variation: Add a twist of risk to this activity by letting the couple roll a dice to determine how many points the statement is worth. If they get it right, they get that many points, but if they get it wrong, they lose that many points.

Feel-N-Name

Couples sit back to back in chairs, blindfolded. Give one an object. He must feel the object and describe it to his date. He cannot tell his date what it is, but can only describe it in as many details as possible. See which couple can name the most objects in a two-minute time period.

Foreign Dictionary Game

For this game, you will need a foreign language dictionary and a bag of numbered household items for each couple. (The dictionaries can be of different languages.) Each couple's bag should contain the same type of items numbered in the same sequence. One person from each couple holds the bag.

To begin, the person holding the bag on each team selects the first object from the bag and describes it to his date, who is sitting across from him. Make sure she cannot see the object he has selected. After she correctly identifies the object, she must look it up in the foreign language dictionary and shout out the name of it in that language as well as she can pronounce it. The first couple to do so wins that round.

Geography

To start, a person names any country, such as "Poland." The next person must name a country which begins with the last letter in the name of the previous country, in the above example, "D." He might say, for example, "Denmark." The third person must name a country that begins with the last letter of the second country, in the above example, "K." If a player cannot think of a country within 30 seconds, he scores a point against himself. The player with the least amount of points at the end of the game wins.

> **Variation:** This game can also be played using states, cities, or geographical landmarks.

Guess It

Obtain ten items for which your group will guess the size, weight, or amount. Have your group sit in a circle with all ten items in the middle. Allow each person to guess the statistic for each item and then measure, weigh, or count the items to determine whose guess was closest to the correct answer. Following are some examples you could use for this game:

1. Jelly beans in a jar. (How many?)
2. Length of yarn rolled into a ball. (How long?)
3. Page of newspaper. (How many words on the page?)
4. Rose. (How many petals?)

> **Variation:** Prepare gender specific items, and either let guys compete against guys and girls compete against girls, or let a team of guys compete against a

team of girls. The guys could guess male items and the girls guess female items, or for a fun twist, let the guys guess female items and the girls guess male items. Some gender specific items you could use:

Male items:
1. Bicycle tire. (How many pounds of pressure?)
2. Hammer. (How many ounces?)

Female items:
1. Blow dryer. (How many watts, by feeling the air pressure only?)
2. Shade of lipstick. (What is the exact color name, like "Dusty Rose" or "Mocha Delight"?)

If/Then

Each person writes the "if" half of an if/then statement on a piece of paper such as, "If the world were going to end tomorrow, and you knew about it today, then . . ." Place all of the "if" statements in a bag, shake them up, and have everyone select a statement out of the bag which was not his own. Everyone reads the "if" statement to himself and, on another piece of paper, writes a "then" statement that would make sense with that "if" statement such as, "Then I would go fishing until it happened." When everyone is finished with his "then" statement, place all of the "then" statements in a separate bag and return the "if" statements to the first bag. Randomly select a slip from each bag and take turns reading an "if" statement followed by a "then" statement and try to determine who wrote each statement. Some will make sense, and some will not; this is a great game for some good laughs!

Initials

Begin this game by addressing someone by his initials and asking him a question such as, "B.V.T., why didn't you ask me out for last Friday night?" He must answer you by using two or three words that begin with your initials. For the initials "T.L.T.", he could say, "Tried, line tied!" If he answers you with something that makes sense and fits with your initials, he gets to call someone else by her initials and ask her a question. If he cannot think of an answer that fits your initials and makes sense within 30 seconds, throw a tablespoon of water at him and ask someone else a question using the new person's initials.

Mafia

Before playing Mafia, make a set of coded index cards to use with this game. There should be one card for each player in attendance. Mark each card on one side only, so that when players receive their cards, no one else knows what their cards say. Mark one fourth of the total number of cards with a red dot, another fourth of the cards with a green dot, one card with a blue dot, and the rest of the cards with a black dot. [Code: Red = mafia, Green = detectives, Blue = moderator, Black = citizens.] The moderator announces his identity, but all other identities must be kept secret.

To begin play, the moderator instructs all players to close their eyes. (Note: the moderator never closes his eyes, as he is needed throughout the game to give instructions.) The moderator tells the mafia to open their eyes and silently decide on one person to "kill." After they decide on someone, the moderator tells them to close their eyes. The moderator then tells the detectives to open their eyes and silently decide on one person to accuse of being a mafia member. The detectives silently select someone. The moderator silently shakes or nods his head to let the detectives know if they are correct or not. The moderator tells them to close their eyes, and when all eyes are closed, he tells everyone to simultaneously open their eyes. The moderator then announces who is "dead."

The members of the community must make an arrest. The group (minus the moderator) holds a discussion to determine who are the mafia. No one can reveal his or her identity during this discussion. The detectives try to sway the group with the secret knowledge they learned when everyone else's eyes were closed, and the mafia members try to convince the group that it is not them. The whole group must agree on someone to arrest by at least a 50% vote. After they name the person to arrest, that person reveals his identity (mafia, detective, or citizen). Both the arrested person and the "dead" person are out of the game for the next round. Play again, using the same identities, as before. Continue playing until either all mafia members have been arrested or until the mafia members have "killed" everyone else.

Make A Wish

Each person in the group takes a piece of paper and writes one of his or her tangible wishes on it. Put all the papers into a hat, mix them up, and redistribute them so that everyone gets someone else's paper. Give everyone ten minutes to locate an object that resembles or symbolizes the unknown player's wish written on the paper. Stretch your imagination! After ten minutes, gather together again.

Take turns reading the wishes, guessing who you think wrote each wish, and presenting the real owner of each wish with the object chosen to resemble the wish. Players should explain why they chose their particular objects as they present them. Return the objects to their places when you are done with the game.

Mappers

For this game, you will need a road map or an atlas. One person looks at the map and chooses a city on it. He then places the map face up on the lap of the person next to him. This person has his or her eyes closed. He tells this person the name of the city, and the person with the map attempts to point to the city on the map while still closing her eyes. If she touches the city, she scores 25 points. For each finger width she is away from the actual city, however, she scores five points less than 25. If she is five or more finger widths away from the city, she gets no points for that round. The player with the most points at the end of the game wins.

Name That Tune

For this date, you will need the help of a pianist. He should sit at a piano in the room where your group sits, with a piano songbook. Divide the group into two teams and select a starting player from each team. The starting players each sit in a chair in the middle of the room, facing towards the group but away from the piano. They compete to see who can "name that tune" in the least amount of piano notes.

The first player says, "I can name that tune in __ notes" (bid a number). The second player either bids a lower number than player #1 or tells player #1 to "name that tune." If he bids a number lower than player #1, player #1 has the option of bidding lower than player #2's bid or challenging him to "name that tune."

Bidding continues until someone challenges the other to "name that tune." The pianist then plays the specified number of notes out of the song book, and the player tries to name the title of the song. If she names it correctly, her team gets a point. If not, the other team can steal the point by naming the tune. Play as many rounds as you desire, giving a team one point for each song it correctly identifies. The team who scores the most points wins.

Party Faces

Give each player a sheet of aluminum foil. Each person smashes the aluminum foil onto his or her face, carefully attempting to create an exact face mold of himself. When finished, instruct players to set their masks in front of themselves and close their eyes. While their eyes are closed, tape a number to each mask, line them up on a table, and make note of which mask belongs to which person. Let players open their eyes, give them each a sheet of paper and a pencil, and have them look at the masks and try to identify which mask belongs to whom. When everyone is finished guessing, reveal the answers.

Person In A Bag

Each person brings five personal items (such as his toothbrush, a pair of socks, a baseball cap, a bottle of cologne, and a T-shirt) in a paper bag to this date. Let each person choose a bag, look at the contents inside, and try to figure out whose bag she thinks it is and why. Players then take turns announcing to the group whose items she thinks are in her bag and why she chose that person. After everyone has made her guess, the real owners of the items reveal themselves.

Professions

One person names a profession and the fastest one to think of a pun about that profession scores a point. Take turns naming professions, and do not think of a pun for any profession that you name. For example:

>   Doctor: Has a lot of patience.
>   Baker: Rolling in the dough.
>   Farmer: Outstanding in his field.
>   Butcher: A cut above the rest.
>   Shoemaker: Has a lot of sole.

Psychiatrist

To play "Psychiatrist," you need at least two people who don't know the secret to this game, and at least two people that do. The people that don't know the secret are the psychiatrists, and the people that do know the secret are the patients. The goal is for the psychiatrists to figure out the secret, or, "to figure out what is wrong with the patients." (The secret is that everyone is supposed to "be" the person sitting to his right.)

Separate the psychiatrists from the patients (for example, put psychiatrists on one side of the room and patients on the other, or sit patients in a circle and put the psychiatrists in the middle of the circle). The psychiatrists randomly ask the patients questions. A patient can either answer what would be the truth if he were the person sitting to his right, or he can answer what would be a lie if he were the person sitting to his right. If he tells the truth, the game continues with another question. However, if he tells a lie, then all the patients yell "Psychiatrist!" and switch places with each other before the psychiatrists can ask another patient a question.

A hint you may want to give your psychiatrists is to ask personal questions of the patients such as, "Do you wear glasses?" or "What color is your shirt?" This may help them figure out the secret faster.

> **Variation:** To play this game again after everyone in the group has learned the secret, send two new psychiatrists out of the room while you decide on a new secret. Instead of the patient answering what would be the truth for the person on his right, a patient could answer what would be the truth for the person on his left, what would be the truth for his mother, or what would be the truth for his date.

Ringleader

One player ("it") leaves the room while the others choose a ringleader. The ringleader determines which motions the group will make, and the group must follow the ringleader's lead. As "it" returns, he finds all the players making the same motion, such as patting their left legs with their left hands. About every 10 seconds, the ringleader makes a different motion and everyone follows. The object of the game is for "it" to figure out who the ringleader is. When he does, the ringleader becomes the new "it." Be careful not to give it away by staring too much at the ringleader.

Say What?

Each couple thinks of a few famous phrases or common sayings and writes them on slips of paper. Put all slips of paper in a hat. Let each couple choose a saying from the hat and "translate it" into word definitions which the others must attempt to figure out. For example, a couple might select the phrase, "Don't bite the hand that feeds you" and translate it into, "Under no circumstances gnaw the digits that provide nourishment for the second person singular." Another example might be, "Ten brains divided by five brains is more advantageous than the opposite of lost." (Two heads are better than one.)

Signs

Sit in a circle and have each person choose a sign (a hand or facial movement which can be done quickly, distinctly, and sneakily; for example, wink an eye, wiggle a nose, put tongue in cheek, or scratch an ear). After everyone has selected a sign, show them to each other. Players should memorize as many signs as possible. Don't worry if you can't remember them all at first; you'll learn them as you play.

Choose someone to stand in the middle of the circle and be "it." "It" closes her eyes while the rest of the group decides who will start the game. After deciding, tell "it" that she can open her eyes. The person starting the game passes the sign to another person in the circle by making eye contact with him and making his sign. He accepts the sign by repeating his own sign back to her. He now holds the sign. He passes the sign to someone else by making her sign to her, and she accepts it by making her sign back to him. Play continues in this fashion.

Meanwhile, "it" diligently tries to spot a movement and verbally identify who has the sign. When "it" catches someone, she gets to join the circle and the person she caught is "it" for the next round. Remember that if "it" accuses you of having the sign, and if someone has passed it to you but you have not yet accepted it, you do not have the sign yet, and so you are not caught. "It" must catch the person who is holding the sign.

Skits In A Bag

Divide into teams of two couples per team, and prepare one bag for every two couples. Place 10 funny objects and/or clothing in each bag, such as a Santa hat, a spatula, a magazine, and a football. Give each team 10 minutes to come up with a skit using every item in the bag as a costume or prop. After 10 minutes, take turns presenting the skits to each other. Then, switch bags and play again.

Smart Formulas

Make up your own game of Smart Formulas by giving each person a paper and pencil and letting him think of several smart formulas, which are coded phrases that include words and/or numbers. For example:

> 4 Q in a G = Four quarts in a gallon.
> 18 W on a ST = Eighteen wheels on a semi-truck.
> 12 D of C = Twelve days of Christmas.
> 101 D = One hundred and one Dalmatians.
> 2,000 L under the S = Two thousand leagues under the sea.

After each person has written down a few formulas, read them aloud and let the group figure them out.

Spell It

Someone starts the game by stating a letter of the alphabet. The next person has to state a second letter without completing a word, however small. She must, however, have an actual real word in mind as she adds on her letter, because at any time, another player can challenge her and ask her what word could be spelled with the letters given, including the letter she just gave. She must be able to state a valid word using all letters given, or she scores a point against herself for that round. Whoever first forms a word scores a point against herself. The person with the least amount of points at the end of the game wins.

Spelldown

Divide into at least two teams. Create a set of alphabet cards for each team on pieces of heavy paper, one piece of paper for each letter. Teams divide the cards among themselves so that everyone has at least one or two cards with which to play.

To play, a mediator calls out a word such as "Apricot." Team members race to spell "apricot" by lining up in order, holding the necessary cards on their chests to form the word. The team which first spells the word correctly scores a point. To make this more challenging, use words which are easy to misspell such as "supersede," "ptarmigan," or "phylactery."

Tap

Players lay in a circle on their stomachs with their heads facing inward, resting on their elbows. They put their hands in front of them, palms down, in between the hands of the people to their left and right. This creates a somewhat mesmerizing circle of hands, and it can be difficult to tell whose hands are whose. One person starts the game by tapping his hand once. The next hand to the right of the first hand must then tap once, and so on. If someone chooses to tap twice instead of once, the direction of the tapping reverses. When someone messes up, he is out of the game and must withdraw from the circle. Play until only two people remain.

That's Me!

This is a great get to know you game. Give each person five index cards and a pencil. He writes one fact about himself on each card (such as, "I love to go camping."). Put all the cards into a hat. Select one card and read it aloud. The person who wrote it jumps up and says, "That's me!" and then sits down. Read the rest of the cards in this manner. After all the cards have been read aloud, give each player a piece of paper. From memory, they must write down as many people's names as they can remember, and as many facts about each person as they can remember. Each name counts as one point, and each fact assigned to the correct participant is worth one point. The person with the most points wins.

Triangle Game

For this game, one person knows the trick and lets the other players figure it out. Make up an imaginary triangle and tell everyone how it is formed. For example, you could say, "There is a triangle and it goes from my nose to the corner of the couch to the light on the ceiling. Whose is it?" Then you must listen closely, because the next person that speaks owns the triangle. (That is the trick.)

Players try to figure out who owns the triangle without knowing what the trick is. They might try to use mathematics, calculated guesses, and other methods before guessing or giving up. When players finish guessing, tell them to whom the triangle belongs. Play the game until players figure out the trick or until you tell it to them.

Twenty!

In this verbal game, everyone is on the same team. Players take random turns trying to count to 20 without ever having two people speak at the same time. To start, one person says, "One." Then, someone else says, "Two," and so on. During the game, every player must speak at least once. If two people say a number at the same time, you must start counting over. If you get good enough to count to 20 easily in this manner, count faster.

Twenty Questions

One person thinks of an object (person, place, or animal). The others in the group take turns asking this player questions about the object that can be answered with either a "Yes" or a "No" only, in an attempt to gain clues and figure out what the object is. The group has 20 questions total in which to figure it out. If someone in the group guesses the object in 20 questions or less, the group scores a point. If no one guesses it correctly after 20 questions have been asked, the player who thought of the object scores a point.

Word

Give each person a sheet of paper and a pencil. Each player draws a large square on her paper, and then divides it into 25 smaller squares by making five horizontal lines and 5 vertical lines within the large square. To play, take turns naming a letter of the alphabet. As it is named, all players write the letter in any one of his squares. Letters cannot be moved to another square once they have been placed, so they must be placed strategically. After all 25 squares contain letters, players try to form as many words as possible. Words can be formed across, down, and diagonally. After five minutes, players count the number of words they have formed and score one point for every letter of every valid word. The player with the most points wins.

CHAPTER THREE

Group Dates On Location

Add Up

Play this game in the car while traveling somewhere with your group. Divide into two teams. As a car passes by heading the opposite direction, observe its license plate number. Team #1 gets the first number and Team #2 gets the last number. Add the number of each passing car. The first team to add up to exactly 100 wins. If a team goes over 100, it must drop back down to 75 and try again.

Air Show

On the day of an air show at an airport or air base in your area, purchase tickets for your group and go watch the show. It's a great way to view some incredible stunts and air maneuvers. For a free version of this date, get a lawn chair for each person in your group and sit outside of the airport. Watch the air show while sitting in your lawn chairs. You could pack a picnic lunch and eat it while you watch the show.

Airport Welcome Committee

Using butcher paper, poster board, and paint, make bright banners and posters with cheery sayings on them such as, "Welcome home!" or "We missed you!" Take your signs to a public airport and welcome total strangers as they get off their airplanes. You may want to video the reactions of the strangers to watch later.

Alpine Slide

In mountainous regions, ski resorts often open for the summer offering fun activities for their summer slopes, such as alpine sliding. Alpine sliding is a great group date. The ski lift or tram takes you to the top of the mountain and you ride down a smooth cement slide on a racing sled. Be sure to follow any precautions or instructions given by the resort in order to protect you from injury while on the track.

April Fooling

Plan and carry out the following harmless, humorous April Fool's joke on your dates on April Fool's Day. (Prior to this date, notify the waiter so he can play along.) Go to dinner together and when it comes time to pay, the guys reach for their wallets, get a horrified look on their faces, and start whispering to each other. After the suspense has mounted, they announce to their dates that they have all accidentally left their money at home. (The girls might offer to pay if they have money with them, but the guys insist that they would rather wash dishes at the restaurant to pay for the meal than have the girls pay for it.) The waiter suggests that the guys follow him to arrange with the manager to wash dishes as payment for the meal. After a few minutes of teasing, the guys pull out their money and announce, "April Fool's!"

Auction

Attend an auction together. As couples, make secret bids on the items for sale, before the auctioneer actually sells each item. Keep track of your bids, because the couple that bids the closest to the actual selling price of each item scores a point.

Board Games In A Tent

Set up a tent outside in the backyard and play board games in the tent. Use a lantern for light. Eat snacks while you play.

Campfire Stories

Sit around a campfire in the mountains and tell stories to each other. Good campfire stories might come from pioneer journals, from personal journals, or from the *Reader's Digest*. Prior to the date, encourage each couple to bring at least one story to share.

Candlelight Dinner

Prior to this date, get permission from the land owner to set up a formal candlelight dinner for your group in the middle of a field, pasture, desert, or beach. Include a table and tablecloth, chairs, a dinner bell, candles, fine china, and soft music playing from a portable CD or cassette player. Arrange for someone dressed as a waiter to hide in a vehicle at the location with your food.

On the night of the date, wear formal attire, drive to the selected location, and enjoy your exquisite setting. After sitting at the table for a few minutes, ring the dinner bell and your waiter or waitress suddenly appears to serve your meal.

Cereal At Sunset

Put several boxes of breakfast cereal in the trunk of your car along with a cooler of milk. Just before the sun sets, take your group to a location with a good view of the western horizon. Set up a card table and folding chairs and give each couple a homemade menu listing the types of breakfast cereal you brought. Let everyone order the type of cereal they'd like to eat. Serve the cereal and eat together as you watch the sunset.

> **Variation:** Do this date during the early hours of the morning and watch the sunrise together instead of the sunset.

Christmas Lights

During the Christmas season, enjoy the festive Christmas lights together. Walk or drive through town together and look at the Christmas lights and decorations. Some cities decorate a special street such as Main Street, so be sure to include that street on your tour.

> **Variation:** Hang Christmas lights at one of your houses together.

Christmas Tree Decorating

In early December, go shopping together for a Christmas tree. After you have purchased a tree, take it to someone's home and decorate it as a group.

> **Variation:** Buy the Christmas tree for a needy family and secretly deliver it to the family along with a box of Christmas lights and other tree decorations.

Circus

Oftentimes, both large and small traveling circuses visit cities and provide all kinds of fun entertainment. When you hear of a circus coming to town, purchase tickets and go together as a group. Make it a fun memory by taking group pictures with the clowns, strong men, snakes, or tigers.

> **Variation:** Attend a traveling carnival together while it is set up in your town.

Climbing Gym

Before planning this group date, make sure everyone in the group can meet the physical challenge of climbing and doesn't have a fear of heights. Go with your group to a climbing gym and practice climbing together. Teach each other skills and learn how to climb the different walls and obstacles provided.

Cornfield Capture The Flag

Sometime in the fall, with permission of the owner of the cornfield, play Capture The Flag in a harvested cornfield. Divide the cornfield in half, using a bandanna on the top of a corn stalk as a visual marker. Split the group into two or more teams, keeping couples together on the same team with the rule that they must stay together during the game. Give each team a bandanna to use as a team flag, a different colored flag for each team. Each team should place its bandanna visibly on its side of the field where it can be defended.

The object of the game is for couples to sneak onto the enemy's side and capture the enemy's flag and return it to their side of the field without being tagged by the enemy while on the enemy's side. If tagged, the couple is placed in a designated prison on the enemy's side and can only be set free by being tagged by another couple from its own team. If a team member is successful in getting the flag but gets caught by the enemy team while running back to his own side, he drops the flag where he was caught and is taken to the enemy's prison. Play continues with the flag in the new location.

Crazy Chain

Loosely tie everyone's hands together in a chain and then either go shopping, take a scenic walk, or go on a picnic together. If being tied together is uncomfortable or dangerous, hold hands instead.

> **Variation:** Blindfold everyone except a leader, who leads the chain. Take turns being the leader.

Cross Country Skiing

Rent or borrow a set of cross country skis for each member of your group and go on a cross country ski excursion in an approved location. Tailor the course to the skill of the group. Be sure to heed all trail warnings and take plenty of water and high energy snacks with you. Let someone know where you'll be going in advance, so you can be contacted if needed.

"Dear" Hunting

For this group date, the girls will send their dates on a "dear hunting" treasure hunt. Get together with your group to (supposedly) play some games and have a party. Suddenly, one of the girls throws an envelope on the floor and all the girls run out the front door. They start the engines of their cars and drive away. The guys will stand bewildered until they open the envelope the girls left them, which says,

> The party was quite fun, we're sure, but we thought we'd spice it up
> By having you get in your cars and go on a treasure hunt.
> Just drive around and follow the clues, it's a good time if you dare,
> And when you make it to the end, we'll have a party there!

The poem should be followed by clue #1, which gives the guys a location to which they must go. When they arrive there, they will find another envelope with clue #2 inside it. The guys must continue to follow the clues until they find their dates at the new party location.

Variation: Rather than giving written clues as to where to go, give the guys photographs of the places instead. Before the date, drive to several places around town that you want your dates to go during this treasure hunt. Take pictures of these locations, and then develop the film. You will give photo #1 to your dates, and have photo #2 waiting for them at location #1. Your dates must look at photo #1, determine where it is, drive there, and find photo #2. Continue in this pattern to the end of the treasure hunt, where you are waiting for your dates with food and games.

Deep Sea Fishing

This group date may not be for everyone, but if you enjoy deep sea fishing, make a date out of it with friends. Charter a boat and experience the excitement of trolling for sailfish, marlin, tuna, or whatever you're after. Take along a camera or video camera to catch the excitement on film.

If the fishing is slow, enjoy the boat ride while you talk or play games.

Demolition Derby

Attending a demolition derby is an unforgettable event. Demolition derbys aren't as common as they used to be, but they do still exist. As a group or as couples, pick a favorite car and driver which you hope will win the derby, and follow it closely throughout the contest. Enjoy the rare scene of watching cars smash into each other—legally!

Digital Photo Shoot

Take one or two digital cameras and go to fun places around town posing for the camera and taking pictures of each other. When you are finished, go back to the house, view the pictures on a computer, and select the ones you want to print. You may even want to use a photo editing program to put your group pictures on the "covers" of magazines, calendars, and stationery before printing them out.

Dinner Hike

For this group date, plan an early evening hike. Somewhere along the way, stop for a rest, build a fire, and cook some hot dogs for dinner. (Be sure that fires are permitted in the area.) Take flashlights with you on the hike in case it gets dark while you are hiking back.

> **Variation:** Plan a surprise dinner hike. Prior to the date, hide a cooler of food somewhere along the hike and during the hike, make some small talk about how it would be nice to have dinner and a cold drink. When you arrive at the cooler, "discover" it.

Dinner On A Train

As a group, invite your dates to dinner but instead of taking them to a regular restaurant, surprise them with a more "moving" experience. Drive to the train station and board the train. Go to the dinner compartment and eat dinner together while enjoying the excitement of riding a train. If convenient, plan and participate in a fun activity at your destination, and then ride the train back home.

Dinner Theater

Locate a place in your area which hosts dinner theaters and go with your group. Enjoy the live performance while you eat your meal together.

Display A Date

Arrange with a store owner or manager to borrow its street-front window display area and set up a romantic dinner there, in full view of the public. As you eat, wave to the people walking by or act like professional models modeling the latest eating techniques.

Double-Handed Bowling

As a group, go bowling together at a local bowling alley. Connect each couple at the hands by tying one hand each together at the wrists. Couples must bowl this way as teams. You may want to ask the bowling alley management to provide your lane with bumper pads if you don't bowl too successfully this way at first.

Drive-In Restaurant

Go to a drive-in restaurant in a pickup truck and have a candlelight dinner in the back of the truck. If there isn't a drive-in restaurant in your area, drive through a fast food restaurant to buy your food, and then have a candlelight dinner in the parking lot.

Driving Movie

Invite your group to a driving movie. Many large vehicles now come equipped with a TV/VCR unit in them, or portable TV/VCR units can be purchased or rented and plugged into the cigarette lighter of the vehicle for power. Drive to the parking lot of a movie theater or another fun location, park the car, and watch the movie together while you are in the car. You might want to bring popcorn, drinks, and other snacks to eat during the show.

Duck Pond Date

For a relaxing date, take your group to a pond and feed the ducks. Ducks usually like bits of bread. Pick a duck and see if you can successfully feed it without the other ducks stealing the food you have thrown to it. You could even take some small children with you and let them feed the ducks too.

Easter Egging

Select and contact a couple of families in your area that have small children and ask their permission to "Easter Egg" their house on Easter Eve. Explain that "Easter Egging" is to boil and dye Easter eggs and hide them in their yard while their children are asleep, so that the children can have a surprise Easter egg hunt from the Easter Bunny on Easter morning. After you get permission from the families, purchase several dozen eggs, boil them, and dye or paint them together as a group. Then on Easter Eve, quietly go to the homes after dark and hide the eggs in the families' yards.

Fashion Show Scavenger Hunt

For this fashionable activity, each couple needs a vehicle and a video camera. Also, some advance preparation by you is necessary for this date. Meet together at someone's house and explain that you're all going on a fashion show scavenger hunt. Give each couple its first envelope which contains the location to which they first must drive (such as one of their own homes). When they get to the location, they find another envelope which instructs them to each dress in a specific type of outfit (such as one from the 1970's.) When they are fully dressed in the outfits, they must take turns modeling for the video camera while the other one videotapes them, and then change back into their normal clothes. In the envelope at that location is also the name of location #2, to which they must then drive.

Each couple must go to the same amount of places with about equal driving distances between them. Couples can even go to the same places on a rotating basis. Every location and outfit must be documented on video. The winning couple is the first couple to meet back at the original meeting place with videotaped footage from all locations. Pop some popcorn and watch the videos together afterwards.

Fast Food Card Game

With permission of the manager of a fast food establishment, take your group to a fast food dinner establishment for food and games. Order your food, eat, and after you eat, play a card game or a board game together at a table in the restaurant. Try not to be too loud or disturbing to the other customers. It might be best to do this activity when the restaurant isn't very crowded and your table isn't needed by another patron.

Fast Food Formal

With permission of the manager of a fast food establishment, surprise your date with a formal table setting at an informal fast food restaurant. Include a tablecloth, glass plates, goblets, nice silverware, linen napkins, and a rose in a vase. After ordering your meal, eat it together in your formal atmosphere.

Fine Arts

As a group, attend a performance of fine arts such as a concert, a symphony, a musical, a play, or a ballet.

Fireworks

Attend a fireworks show together. For a fun game during the show, take turns guessing which color the next firework is going to be. Whoever is right scores a point. Afterwards, you could buy your own fireworks and light them together. Be sure they are legal in your state, and obey all fire restrictions.

Fishing

Fishing as a group can be great fun. Try to determine where and what the fish are biting before you go, so you can go prepared. If you catch some fish and it is legal to keep them, cook and eat them together.

Flea Market

Prior to the date, check a newspaper for an upcoming flea market in your vicinity. Go to the flea market together and enjoy looking at the interesting things for sale. You could give each couple a challenge to split up and see who can find the best deal on a given item.

Flipper Tennis

Play tennis in diving flippers. For more advanced players, add goggles or a snorkeling mask to the tennis attire. Play both singles and doubles. Since movements are much slower than in normal tennis, you might even want to play in triplets. Take turns videotaping the game for later laughs.

Four Wheeling

Go four wheeling as a group, either in a four wheel drive truck or on four wheel all terrain vehicles. Plan your trip in advance and make a picnic out of it. Take some form of communication with you in case you get stuck, break down, or have an emergency. Be safe, and adapt your trip to everyone's level of comfort and skill.

Funny Interviews

Go to a public place such as a shopping mall and give each couple a tape recorder hooked to a microphone or a video camera. Go around interviewing willing strangers, recording their answers to your questions. You could ask them questions about anything you want, from real political issues to hypothetical situations to what types of things they enjoy. When each couple has completed asking a set number of questions, meet back together and listen and laugh to the tapes you have made.

Halloween Ghosting

About two weeks before Halloween, make and bake Halloween sugar cookies together. Use Halloween character cookie cutters such as ghosts, witches, and bats and frost the cookies with your favorite frosting. Afterward, go Halloween Ghosting by leaving a plate of cookies on the doorstep of someone you care about. Ring the doorbell and run, trying to not be discovered. With the plate of cookies, leave a note stating that the family has just been spooked by the Halloween Ghost. They should return the favor by baking cookies for and "spooking" two more families on the following day. Also leave a white paper ghost on their door as an indicator that they have been "spooked" by the Halloween Ghost. If every family that gets "spooked" spooks two families each within 24 hours, it is amazing how many families will receive a plate of goodies before Halloween.

Haunted House

Sometime during the month of October, attend a haunted house together. In many areas, there are often free spook alleys sponsored by either community organizations or families that you could attend as well.

Helicopter Ride

This group date is definitely out of the ordinary. As a group, charter a helicopter and take a helicopter ride together.

Holiday Date

This date can be done at any holiday of the year. Dress up as the holiday dictates and, with video camera in hand, interview willing strangers on tape, asking them what they know about the origin and purpose of the holiday.

Horse And Buggy Ride

Many cities offer horse and buggy rides through a scenic or historic area. Split the fare between the couples in your group and enjoy the ride.

Variation: For a winter activity, arrange to ride in a horse-drawn sleigh.

Horseback Riding

Prior to this date, contact a horse owner and arrange to ride his horses for this group date, or rent some riding horses for your group. Find a good location to ride horses together. If you don't have enough horses for everyone to ride his or her own, ride double as couples. Take a picnic lunch along and when you find a suitable spot, tie the horses, spread out a picnic blanket, and eat together. If possible, you might actually pick up your dates on horses rather than in cars.

Hospital Visits

Visit patients in a hospital. Read to them, perform musical numbers, do a puppet show for hospitalized children, or just talk to the patients.

Variation: Make finger puppets for hospitalized children. Perform a puppet show for them with the finger puppets and then give the finger puppets to the children before you leave.

Hot Air Balloon Ride

As a group, rent a hot air balloon and pilot to take you on a scenic ride over the countryside. Split the cost between couples.

Hunting

Go hunting together as a group. Only those who carry guns and do the shooting will need a license and stamps or tags. Others can help spot, flush, carry, skin, butcher, and preserve the game. Be careful to follow all hunting safety rules, and never kill anything unless you plan to eat it.

Ice Fishing

Check with a local sporting goods store to determine the location of a good ice fishing area and what baits to use there. Be sure to let everyone know the plan in advance so that they can dress appropriately. Take plenty of hot chocolate and snacks with you and if possible, erect a tent or other shelter over your ice hole. Before you go, make sure you are licensed to fish and check with the Fish and Game department to verify that the ice will be thick enough to support you.

Ice Skating

Rent or borrow ice skates for everyone in the group, and go ice skating together at a public ice skating rink. Teach each other skating techniques and practice them together. Expect slips and falls. After skating, make and drink some hot chocolate to warm up.

> **Variation:** If there are ponds in the area that have been designated as safe for ice skating, ice skate on the frozen pond. Bring along a portable CD or cassette player if you want to play music while you skate.

Laser Tag

Laser tag is a high-tech, suspenseful activity. Go to a laser tag establishment and play a few rounds of laser tag together, competing as couples or as teams.

Laundromat Date

Go with another couple to a local Laundromat and do

GROUP DATES ON LOCATION

your laundry together. While the laundry is washing and drying, play card games or board games. You may also want to take a CD or cassette player along and listen to music while you wait for your clothes.

Luck Walk

Go to a safe neighborhood, town, or shopping mall where there are many corners or intersections and choose a target location where you want to end up after 45 minutes. Start walking together as a group. Each couple flips a coin at every corner. Heads means turn right, tails means turn left. Couples have a 50% chance of separating from the other couples at the first corner. After 45 minutes, each couple writes down the location of where they are and then meets the others at the target location to determine who was closest to the target location when the time had expired. That couple wins.

Meals On Wheels

Go out to eat together as a group but instead of using a car for transportation, ride bicycles, ride unicycles, or skate on roller blades.

Mountain Biking

For this group date, go mountain biking together. In advance, pick a trail that is suited to the skills of the group, then enjoy each other's company as you bike along the trail. Take plenty of water and if you want to, take a picnic along and eat it somewhere along the way.

Outdoor Movie

Before this date, check the weather forecast to make sure it won't rain on you for this activity. On a nice, clear night, set up a TV/VCR outside on the dry ground. Place bean bag chairs, cushions, or a trampoline near the screen. Pop popcorn, get comfortable, and watch a movie together outside.

Paint-Ball

Reserve time at a paint-ball gallery and play paint-ball as a group. Paint-ball galleries are usually set up with mazes, towers, sawdust flooring, and other features. They also provide referees, ammunition, and protective gear which add to the experience. It can sting to be hit by a paint-ball fired from a paint-ball gun, so make sure everyone in the group is aware of the risks, uses caution, and is a willing participant.

> **Variation:** Buy, borrow, or rent paint-ball equipment and play paint-ball outdoors. Wear protective eye and head gear and protective padding or thick layers of clothing. Play as couples or teams, and try playing different types of games such as Capture The Flag, Capture The Queen, or Total Elimination.

> **Variation:** Instead of using paint-ball guns, buy paint-balls and use slingshots to fire them. Slingshots aren't usually as forceful as paint-ball guns, but still provide enough force for a paint-ball to break on impact. They're often more difficult to aim than a paint-ball gun, as well. Therefore, teams can play in closer vicinity with less cover and can make reasonable strategic maneuvers without as much risk of getting hit as easily. Of course, the protective gear mentioned earlier still applies.

Photograph Scavenger Hunt

For this date, give each couple a camera and a list of things each couple must photograph within a given time frame. The list should include several things the couples must do, such as wade in a pond, hug a statue, and push a crosswalk button. At the "Go" signal, couples race around town, find the items on their lists, and take the necessary pictures.

If your group uses instant cameras, simply bring the photos back for judging; if you use regular cameras, develop the film at a one-hour film lab; if you use digital cameras, print the photos using your computer and printer. Give an award to the first couple that returns with all of the required pictures.

Planetarium

Planetariums often feature laser shows or educational programs about the solar system. Some planetariums also offer fascinating outer space exhibits. Call in advance to see what's playing, and then go to a planetarium together and enjoy the show.

Rappelling

If everyone in your group is willing and able, get your climbing ropes and other gear together and go rock climbing and rappelling together. Be sure to wear all required safety equipment, follow all safety rules, and do not exceed the skill level of anyone in the group.

Recipe Book Scavenger Hunt

Divide into teams and go on a scavenger hunt to obtain favorite recipes from neighbors. Race to see who can get the most recipes in a given period of time. Each recipe must be handwritten by a member of your group. After an allotted amount of time, go back to someone's house and count recipes to see who obtained the most.

After the hunt, compile a recipe book with all of the recipes you have obtained. Divide the book into sections such as appetizers, salads, breads, main dishes, desserts, and beverages. Be sure to credit each recipe to the neighbor who contributed it to you. Make a copy of the book for everyone in your group. You might also give a copy of the recipe book to each person that contributed a recipe to your cause.

Regressive Dinner
Begin this date by eating dessert at the first person's home. Then drive to someone else's house for the main course, and finish at a third person's home with the appetizer.

Religious Service
With your group, visit the religious services of a religious group in your community. Afterward, go somewhere else and discuss your religious beliefs as a group. Be careful to be respectful of the services as well as of each other's beliefs.

Remote Control Car Races
Each couple should bring a working remote control car to this date (and maybe some extra batteries). Create a race track on which the cars will have to race, including several obstacles that the cars must get through. Couples set their cars on the starting line and wait for the "Go!" signal to begin the race. Each couple must control its car as a couple—the boy controlling the left and right motions and the girl controlling the forward and backward motions, or vice versa. The car that reaches the finish line first wins.

> **Variation:** Play Remote Control Car Tag. Designate one car to be "it." "It" chases and tries to tag the other cars. When a car gets tagged, it becomes the new "it." Designate boundary lines if necessary.

Restaurant Progressive Dinner

Have a group progressive dinner by going to different restaurants for different courses of your meal. At the first restaurant, order an appetizer and eat it. Pay the bill, drive to a different restaurant, and order the main course. Eat, pay the bill, and then drive to the final restaurant for dessert.

> **Variation:** Give each of your dates $25 and tell them that they are in charge of where you go to eat dinner. They must take you to three different places for the three different courses of the meal, and they may not go over budget.

Road Trip

Dress like tourists and go sightseeing to interesting tourist attractions in your area. Take pictures and develop copies for everyone.

Rodeo

It doesn't matter if you're a city slicker or a cowboy, a rodeo can provide great entertainment for all types of people. Go to a rodeo and watch the calf roping, the bronco riding, the barrel racing, the clowns, and the other exciting events.

S.W.A.T.

Each participant becomes a member of the "S.W.A.T. Team." "S.W.A.T." stands for "Service Without A Trace," and during this date, you will look for secret service opportunities and try to carry them out without being detected. For example, you could drive around the neighborhood with shovels, rakes, and other tools in the trunk and secretly rake people's leaves, sweep their driveways, or shovel the snow from their sidewalks or driveways. As you leave a house after serving the people who live there, you could leave a card on the doorstep that says, "Service For You by the S.W.A.T. (Service Without A Trace) Team."

Santa Visit

As a group, go to a shopping mall and visit Santa Claus during the Christmas season. Take a video camera with you. Have a group picture taken with him and take turns sitting on his lap, telling him what you want for Christmas. Videotape the proceedings, and then go to someone's house to watch the video.

Seventies Date

Plan a 1970's group date. For the first part of the date, go with your group to a thrift store and purchase clothing that exemplifies the 1970's era. Wear the 1970's clothes for the remainder of the date and spend the evening listening and dancing to 1970's music.

Signature Scavenger Hunt

Divide your group into teams of about two couples per team, and give each team a list of categories (see below) and a pencil. Teams must go from house to house in the neighborhood searching for people who match the categories listed on their papers, and have those people sign their names next to the categories they fulfill. The teams can only get one signature per household and must return to the starting place at a designated time, finished or not. Give a prize to the team that gets the most signatures within the given time frame. Categories may include such things as:

1. Someone who has dyed her hair a different color.
2. Someone who was born in the same month as a team member.
3. Someone whose last name begins with the same letter as that of a team member.
4. Someone who has been to Hawaii on vacation.
5. Someone who drives a convertible.

Variation: Instead of going out into the neighborhood searching for people to sign the category lists, play this game with your own group. Each player should have a category list and a pencil and must obtain signatures from any other players who fit a category on his list.

Skeet Shooting

Go to a skeet shooting range or an approved wilderness area and shoot clay pigeons with shotguns. If one of your group is particularly skilled in shooting, let him teach you about aim, follow through, and timing. He could also teach you how to throw the clay pigeons with a manual thrower or how to use a spring loaded launcher. Before shooting with or handling the shotguns, however, make sure everyone knows how to handle them safely.

Snowmobiling

Obtain a snowmobile for every couple in your group and go snowmobiling in a designated snowmobiling area together. Ride safely and tailor the course to the level of expertise of those in your group. Take along some hot chocolate and snacks as well as a form of communication in case of trouble or a break down.

Square Dancing

Go to a barn or a decorated gym dressed in Western attire. Hire a good square dance caller to come to this date and teach your group how to square dance.

State Park

Visit a state park. As you enter, use the map of the park to plan out a day of hiking, sightseeing, and taking pictures. Plan your route in such a way that you arrive at rest stops and picnic tables at appropriate times during the day for convenience in washing and eating.

Supercalifragilisticexpialidocious

For this travel game, divide into two teams down the center of the vehicle, with people sitting on the left side of the car on team #1, and people sitting on the right side of the car on team #2. Team #1 uses the signs on the left side of the road and team #2 uses the signs on the right side of the road. At the "Go" signal, teams look at street signs and license plates on their side of the road to find each letter of the word "Supercalifragilisticexpialidocious" in order. The first team to successfully and honestly do so wins. Use paper and pen if needed. Part of the fun is deciding just how the word is spelled before you begin playing the game.

Swing Dancing

Find out where a swing dance is being held or where a good jazz band is playing, and go swing dancing together. Before you go, consider getting someone to teach your group some swing dance steps such as the Jitterbug, so you will feel more comfortable dancing once you get there.

Treat Or Tricking

This date is obviously Trick or Treating backwards, which is exactly what the date entails. On Halloween night, instead of Trick or Treating, take candy around to homes and treat them, thanking them for making children happy on Halloween.

Trivia Scavenger Hunt

Divide into teams of two couples per group and give each team a list of several trivia questions and a pencil. Teams must go from house to house searching for people who can tell them the correct answers to the trivia questions. The teams can get only one answer per household and must return to the starting place at a designated time, finished or not. After the teams return, announce the correct answers to the trivia questions. Award a prize to the team that collected the most correct answers. Some examples of trivia questions you could use are:

1. What do you call a baby kangaroo?
2. In what country would you find the "Blarney Stone?"
3. In the movie *The Princess Bride,* what does Wesley say while rolling down the hill?
4. In what year did Disneyland open?
5. What type of sea creature stuns its prey with sound waves before eating it?

Variation: Instead of asking trivia questions from a wide variety of topics, focus on questions of a single topic such as "Animals," "World Geography," "Religions," "Music Groups," "Automobiles," or "Movies."

Weed Salad

Using the *Boy Scout Handbook* or other reliable source, find out what local weeds are edible. Stroll through the countryside collecting edible weeds. A cooler with ice and/or water will help keep the weeds fresh until you get home. After your walk, return to someone's home and prepare a large weed salad to share.

Where Are We?

Get in a vehicle with enough seatbelts for everyone in your group. Have everyone except the driver close her eyes or wear a blindfold. The driver drives the car somewhere while everyone else's eyes remain closed. When the driver announces that you have reached your destination, the passengers must guess where they are. Then they can open their eyes. Switch drivers and begin again.

Your Lucky Date

Prior to this date, take photographs of several different restaurants and several different activities that you might do for this group date. Develop the film and then place the photos in envelopes labeled "restaurants" and "activities." Let one couple choose a photo out of the "restaurants" envelope to determine where you eat, and let another couple choose a photo out of the "activities" envelope to determine what you do for the after-dinner activity.

Zoo

Spend the day at a zoo together, and take a video camera with you. As you walk through the zoo, take video footage of your group and the animals you see. For intellectual fun, assign each couple one of the zoo animals, and have them read about it and become an "expert" for that animal. Then, take turns videoing each other teaching the group about their assigned animals. At the end of the excursion, interview the group on camera, asking them what their favorite animals were and why. Hint: Depending on the size of your group, the zoo may offer you a group discount. Call in advance to find out.

CHAPTER FOUR

Group Dates Involving Water

Beach Golf

Play golf on the sandy beach of an ocean or lake with floating plastic balls, such as whiffle balls (plastic balls with holes in them used for golf and baseball practice). Use cups pushed into the sand for the holes. If you hit a ball into the water, retrieve it.

Beach Kite Flying

The beach is a great place to fly kites, since the breeze coming off the ocean often allows you to launch and fly kites with little or no running. As a group, fly different types of kites, seeing how high you can fly them and what types of tricks or maneuvers you can do. Try flying a two-handled kite with your date.

Beach Picnic

Spend a day at the beach. Eat a picnic lunch, listen to music, play frisbee, build sand castles, fish, canoe, swim, and play horse shoes. If it's allowed, have a barbecue at sunset or build a fire on the shore and tell stories.

GROUP DATES INVOLVING WATER

Variation: If you don't live near a beach, this activity works great at a lake as well.

Canoeing

On a warm summer day, take your dates and some canoes to a lake. If the water is clear, try to spot fish and go fishing if you desire. See how quietly you can paddle, and see how fast you can go. Be sure to wear life jackets. If your group has more than one canoe at this activity, beware of water fights.

Firing Squad

Divide into two teams. Place a strip of masking tape on the ground to make a firing line which cannot be crossed. Each team blindfolds two team members, one of whom sits in a chair four feet in front of the firing line, facing the line. The other stands on the firing line with a fully loaded squirt gun, facing the seated teammate. The rest of the team players line up behind the shooter.

At the "Go" signal, the blindfolded shooter begins squirting water at the person sitting down (the target), attempting to shoot a full stream of water into his opened mouth. Only the target can speak and give directions for aiming to the shooter. When a direct hit into the mouth is achieved, the target person removes his blindfold and escorts the blindfolded shooter to the chair as the next target. Then he gives his blindfold to the next shooter who puts it on and play continues. The team that squirts all of its members in the mouth first wins.

Float-In Movie

Set up a TV/VCR by the side of a home swimming pool, far enough away that it (and any electric cords) won't get wet. Tell everyone to bring a floating device such as a raft, a canoe, or an inner tube. Watch a movie such as *Jaws* together while you're in the pool.

Homemade Water Slide

Make your own water slide out of a heavy sheet of plastic. Lay the sheet of plastic (the slide) out flat on the lawn and soak it with water. Either turn on the sprinklers or leave a hose running on the slide. Dress in swimming suits and run towards the slide. When you reach the slide, jump onto it and slide across it to the other end.

> **Variation:** Play water slide catch. As one person slides across the plastic, throw a soft ball towards her and see if she can catch it.

> **Variation:** Add fine dirt to the water and have a mudslide.

Hot Springs

Hot springs provide fun, natural entertainment almost any time of year. Go as a group to a natural hot spring or go to a hot springs resort which offers naturally heated swimming pools and hot tubs. Don't forget your swimming suits!

Human *Battleship*

In this version of the board game *Battleship,* humans are the battleships and water balloons are the bombs. Play on either side of a wooden privacy fence or other outdoor visual barrier. Make even boundaries on each side of the fence. Each person then chooses a strategic position within the boundaries on his side of the fence and lays down on his

GROUP DATES INVOLVING WATER

back. Players must be at least three feet away from the fence. Once a player selects his position, he cannot move for the duration of the round unless he gets out.

Give each player 5-10 small water balloons to keep next to him as artillery. When everyone is in position, take turns lobbing the water balloons over the fence at each other (while still laying down), trying to hit a human ship on the other side. Players on the team being thrown at should cover their faces with their hands. If a person is hit, he must yell "Hit!" to the other team, and he is sunk for that round. Play until one team has sunk all of the opposing team's ships.

> **Variation:** Have team members represent specific ships (battleships, aircraft carriers, scout ships, submarines, cruisers) by sitting or laying in certain shapes and lengths.

> **Variation:** For a drier version of this activity, use soft foam balls instead of water balloons as artillery.

Jumping Catch

Divide into teams for this date in a swimming pool. Take turns jumping off the diving board. As a person jumps off the diving board, throw her a soft ball and see if she can catch it mid-air. If she does, her team scores one point. The team scores another point if she continues to hold onto it under water until she surfaces again (air-filled balls are especially hard to submerge).

Mirror Splash

Divide into couples for this wet activity. Create a starting line and a finish line on a playing field, and place several obstacles between the lines. One guy sits in a chair at the finish line and holds an empty cup on his head and a mirror in his hand. His back should be towards the starting line. Blindfold his date and give her a full cup of water, which she must hold on top of her head. Position her at the starting line.

At the "Go" signal, her date must look in the mirror and verbally guide her through the maze with his voice. When she reaches him, he instructs her to pour the water from her cup into his cup. Time them to see how long it takes them to finish the race, and measure the amount of water that successfully makes it into his cup. Then it is another couple's turn. Give an award for the couple with the fastest time and the most water in its cup at the end of the race. Note: You may want to videotape the races and watch them together later.

Variation: Divide into teams and blindfold two people from each team. One person from each team sits in a chair at a finish line, holding an empty cup on their heads. At the "Go" signal, a blindfolded member of each team scoops a cup of water out of a pail and runs towards their teammate in the chair. Another teammate holds a mirror in his hand with his back towards the finish line and gives directions to the blindfolded runner to run to the guy in the chair and carefully pour the water from her cup into his cup. When the cup is empty, the blindfolded guy dumps his cup into a bucket at his feet. The runner removes her blindfold and runs it to another teammate who puts it on and runs with a new cup of water. The team that gets the most water in the bucket after every team member has been the runner wins.

Peers On The Pier

This dinner date with your peers takes place on a pier. Set up folding chairs and a card table on a pier and set the table for dinner. With your dates, stroll along the beach watching the sunset, watching the birds, playing frisbee, or even fishing. When you're ready for dinner, walk down the pier and enjoy a seafood dinner while overlooking the ocean and feeling the misty breeze on your faces. Keep the food warm or cold with coolers or food insulators until you're ready to eat.

River Picnic

On a nice day, find a slow, shallow spot in a river or stream and set up folding chairs and a card table right in the water. Take your shoes off, roll up your skirts and pant legs, and sit down to a river picnic. Let your feet cool off in the stream while you enjoy your lunch. Keep drinks, watermelon, and other cold things cool by setting them in a pool of the stream where they won't float away.

River Rafting

Charter a rafting trip with a professional river rafting company. Choose the type of rafting trip you want, either a trip for leisure floating, sightseeing, and fishing or one for white water rafting with rapids and other thrills. Always wear your life jackets and always obey the river guides.

Shark

Designate a person to be the shark for this date in a swimming pool. The shark attempts to catch one of the other people in the pool. The people can get out of the pool for a maximum of five seconds at a time, but the shark cannot ever get out of the pool. The first person caught becomes the new shark.

Slip-Ball

Set this game up as if to play softball, but use a plastic bat and a beach ball instead of real softball equipment. Use children's wading pools for first, second, and third bases, and a wet sheet of black plastic for the stretch from third base to home plate. A batter can choose to either hit the pitched ball with a bat or kick a rolled ball instead. After a successful hit or kick, she runs the bases as in softball, but she must slide home to score. The fielding team gets a runner out by either catching his fly ball, tagging him with the ball, or touching the base he is running to while in possession of the ball before he gets to the base. There are no strikes or strike-outs in this game. Dress for wet.

Snorkeling

Find a safe, clear body of water with visible underwater wildlife that has been approved for snorkeling. Buy, rent, or borrow snorkeling gear, dress in swimming suits, and snorkel together. For safety and help in flotation, some life vests can be worn in a "U" shape around your torso, with the head support under your chest and the two open ends sticking up out of the water above your back. You may want to take an underwater camera and take some pictures of what you see. After you have developed the film, look up the creatures in a book and see what they are.

Spray-O-War

This wet activity requires two hoses, one for each team. Fit each hose with a spray nozzle that projects a strong, straight stream of water. Tie one end of a thin nylon rope above your heads to a tree and thread the loose end of the rope through a plastic ring toy (or any object which will slide easily along the rope when it is struck with the stream of water). Tie the loose end of the rope tightly to another tree, creating a tight, horizontal rope along which the ring can slide when it is sprayed with the water.

To play, divide into two teams and choose one person to be the referee. Teams should stand on opposite sides of the rope. Give the first player on each team one of the hoses. Assign each team an end of the rope to protect. The rest of the teammates line up behind the first player. Slide the ring to the center of the rope.

At the "Go" signal, the first player on each team runs toward the ring, spraying it towards the other team's side of the rope. After 30 seconds, the referee blows a whistle and the sprayers immediately give their hoses to the next players in line. These next players rush to the rope and continue spraying the toy ring. Continue in this fashion until a team successfully sprays the ring over to the other team's end of the rope. Participants should wear goggles or swim masks to protect their eyes from the spraying water. Dress for wet.

Squirts

Everyone sits in a circle. Select someone to be "it" and give "it" a piece of paper, a pencil, and a squirt gun filled with water. "It" names a category such as "The Seven Dwarves" and writes the name of one of the dwarves on her piece of paper without showing anyone. Players in the circle take turns naming one of the dwarves without duplicating someone else's answer. Whoever gives the answer written on "it's" paper gets squirted with water from the squirt gun by "it." That person becomes the new "it."

Swimming Pool Picnic

Dress in swimsuits for this summer group date. Float in a large raft in the middle of a swimming pool. Have airtight containers of food floating in the pool as well, connected to the raft with a piece of fishing line. When you get hungry, pull the food to your group by "reeling" it in. Eat what you want, then seal the lid and set it afloat again.

Water Balloon Volleyball

For this twist to volleyball, put a little bit of water in a balloon and use it instead of a volleyball. The server can either have assists to get the balloon over the net or serve from closer to the net. Regular volleyball rules apply. Have several balloons on hand, as someone is sure to burst the balloon in a "splash" hit.

> **Variation:** To play Balloon Volleyball without water, play volleyball with a regular balloon as the volleyball and add the rule that a team can have up to four hits per side to get the ball over the net.

Water Basketball

For this date in a swimming pool, divide into teams and play Water Basketball using a pool-side basketball hoop and a miniature basketball.

Water Park

Go with your group to a water park and enjoy the slides, pools, and water rides. Where there are multiple slides that start and end in the same place, race down them, having someone judging the race at the bottom of the slide. Eat lunch together at one of the snack stands at the park.

Water Ring Toss

Using a floating ring toss game, play ring toss from the diving board of a swimming pool. Divide into teams, giving each member of the team a ring. As a player jumps off the diving board, he throws his ring, attempting to put it on one of the floating pegs.

Waterskiing

Go with your group to a suitable body of water and go waterskiing together. Be sure to obey all laws and regulations. Take some food along and have a picnic in the boat or on the shore when you get hungry.

> **Variation:** Rent and ride jet skis or wave runners together.

CHAPTER FIVE

Group Dates Around A Table

Balcony Barbecue

On a warm summer evening, set up a barbecue grill, a card table, and some folding chairs on your balcony. Cook and eat dinner together at the table on the balcony.

Big Mouths

This activity is a contest to see which couple at your party can stuff the most marshmallows into its mouths. Sit at a table with bags of marshmallows in the middle of the table. Take turns stuffing marshmallows into your mouths, counting them as you go. Participants cannot chew or swallow the marshmallows, and they must be able to close their lips all the way with no white showing. Couples play as teams, and each marshmallow is worth one point, so combine the amount of marshmallows in his mouth with the amount in her mouth to determine how many points that couple receives. The couple with the most points wins a prize.

Birthday Surprise

On a friend's birthday, throw a surprise "This Is Your Life" group date in her honor. Prior to the date, gather interesting information from her family to share during the date. Have several couples hiding at your house when she arrives there, unsuspecting, with her date. Yell, "Surprise!" as she enters and tell her the date is in honor of her birthday.

During the party, show home movies or slides of her as a child, play her favorite childhood games, sing her favorite childhood songs, and eat her favorite childhood foods. Wear party hats and other birthday regalia and eat cake and ice cream around the birthday table.

Blindfolded Play Dough Sculpting

Each person needs a blindfold and each couple needs some play dough for this group date. Put a bunch of household objects in a bag such as a flyswatter, a toothbrush, and a calculator. Everyone puts on his blindfold and selects one object out of the bag. With a clump of play dough, couples try to sculpt the object out of play dough together. When a couple finishes its sculpture, they remove their blindfolds and admire their masterpiece.

Following is a recipe for making homemade play dough:

1 cup flour	1 cup water
1 tablespoon oil	1/2 cup salt
1 teaspoon cream of tartar	food coloring

Mix ingredients in a pan. Cook over medium heat until mixture pulls away from the sides of the pan and becomes doughy in consistency. Knead until cool. Keeps 3 months unrefrigerated in an airtight container.

Breakfast Party

Invite your group to a morning date of cooking breakfast together. As a group, prepare a delicious breakfast that might include bacon, eggs, pancakes, cereal, fresh fruit, waffles, fruit juice, milk, or hot chocolate. Each couple could be in charge of bringing some of the ingredients and of cooking part of the meal. When everything is ready, sit down and eat together. Clean up together after you are done.

Variation: Have the girls cook for the guys or the guys cook for the girls.

Cake Decorating

Bake cakes together, one cake per couple. When the cakes have baked and cooled, each couple sits at a table and decorates its cake. When you are finished, you could eat the cakes or deliver them to families in the area who are in need of special cheer.

Candy Making

Make homemade candy. Prepare in advance by deciding which candies to make and making sure you have all of the necessary ingredients on hand to make them. After making the goodies, eat some and then deliver some to family, friends, and neighbors.

Canning

Plan this date well enough in advance to know what fruits or vegetables are available in the current season. Harvest the food yourselves or buy it from a fruit and vegetable stand. Get glass jars, lids, rings, a canner, and instructions. Follow current canning guidelines to properly preserve the produce.

GROUP DATES AROUND A TABLE

Clay Sculpting

Give each person a block of good clay, which he will use to sculpt his date's face. Guys sculpt girls' faces, and then girls sculpt guys' faces. When the date is over, everyone gets to take home an original sculpture made by his or her date.

Collages And Cookies

For this group date, you will need several old magazines that can be cut up. Begin by making a batch of cookie dough together. Then, as the cookies bake in the oven, everyone sits at a table and looks through the magazines searching for photographs, phrases, or words that describe his or her date. Look for things that describe your date's personality, looks, talents, hobbies, and character. Cut out these words, phrases, and pictures and glue them to a piece of posterboard, making a collage. After everyone finishes making a collage, and after your cookies are done, eat cookies while you take turns explaining your collage to the group and presenting it to your date.

> **Variation:** Instead of each person making a collage about his date, make one collage together per couple. The collage should describe each other as well as your relationship or feelings for each other.

Creative Cookery

Give each couple a sack filled with several ingredients that could be used to make a meal. You can choose to include or leave out a recipe. Couples should prepare a meal together from the ingredients found in their sacks. Then sit around a table and eat your meals together.

Variation: Each couple brings a sack of ingredients to this date and exchanges sacks with another couple, so no one has the sack he brought to the date. Prepare meals as couples from the sacks, and then sit around a table and eat.

Dinner And Olympics

Once every two years, you can enjoy either the Summer or Winter Olympic Games. With your group, decide on a foreign meal to cook together, find a recipe for it, and purchase the necessary groceries. Cook the meal as a group and eat it as you watch the Olympic Games together on television.

Eating Contest

Hold an eating contest to see which member of the group can eat the largest quantity of jalapeño peppers, pickled pigs feet, or other interesting food item. Or, hold a drinking contest to see who can chug a bottle of root beer the fastest. Give this drinking contest a twist by putting the beverage in baby bottles and race to see who can suck the bottle dry the fastest.

Flour Faces

Firmly pack some flour into a cup, turn the cup upside down, and carefully slide the cup off the solid mound of flour. Gently set a coin vertically on top of the mound of flour. Take turns cutting away slices of the flour with a butter knife, trying not to make the coin fall over or the mound collapse. Whoever makes the coin fall or the mound collapse must retrieve the coin with his mouth. Take pictures for fun memories.

Halloween With The Elderly
Bring elderly people to your house and let them pass out candy to the children who come to your door. Play a game with them in between trick or treaters.

Homemade Ice Cream
Assign couples to bring the different ingredients needed to make homemade ice cream. Make homemade ice cream using an older hand cranked mixer or a modern electric mixer (the hand cranked ones provide more interaction). When the ice cream is done, enjoy eating it together.

Hunter and Hunted
Blindfold a couple. One of them is the hunter and the other is the hunted. Place them at opposite ends of a table. At the signal, the hunter attempts to sneak around the table and catch the hunted, while the hunted attempts to detect his movements and avoid him by moving the opposite way around the table. Both the hunter and the hunted must keep a hand on the edge of the table at all times. Time the game so that if the hunted isn't caught within the allotted time, the hunted wins.

International Dinner
Prior to this date, assign each couple a country. They should prepare and bring a large dish of food from that country, come to the date dressed like natives of that country, and bring interesting artifacts from that country, if possible. For the date, sit around a table and eat the different foods while you take turns teaching each other about the countries you were assigned.

Jewelry Making

Make jewelry together. If possible, let each couple come prepared to teach the others how to make a jewelry item. You could make rings, braided necklaces, leather jewelry, or beaded earrings, for example.

Magazine Scavenger Hunt

For this date, ask each couple to bring a bunch of old magazines. Sit around a table and put the pile of magazines in the middle of the table. Call out an item such as "cologne" or "beach," and let the couples race to find a picture of the item in one of the magazines. The couple that finds the picture first scores a point.

Murder Mystery Party

A few weeks before this date, buy, borrow, or rent a murder mystery game (such as *How To Host A Murder*) from a store that sells board games. Follow the instructions inside the game box to prepare to host a murder mystery party. Most likely, you will need to cast parts, assign part of a meal to each couple, and mail invitations to your guests. Give your guests 1-2 weeks notice before the party to locate costumes and plan to be in attendance. Then, on the night of the date, have fun eating a meal together and playing parts in a game to solve a fictional murder mystery!

Pizza Party

Make homemade pizzas as couples. Provide the dough and the sauce, and ask each couple to bring a few toppings to share (i.e. cheese, sausage, pepperoni, ham, pineapple, black olives, mushrooms, peppers, onions). Couples roll out their own crusts and design their own pizzas. See who can come up with the most unusual or attractive pizzas. Cook and eat them together.

Progressive Story Writing

Give each person a blank piece of paper and a pencil and have everyone sit at a table. Players begin writing a story on their papers. After three minutes, everyone passes her story one person to the left, reads the story she just received, and continues writing the next part of the new story on the new paper. Continue in this fashion, switching papers every three minutes, until everyone has written a section of every story. Be sure that the last person to write on a story writes a conclusion for it. Then, read the stories aloud to each other.

Rotating Cards

Set up folding chairs and card tables with card games on them that are familiar to the group such as *Rook, Uno, Phase 10,* and *Skip Bo.* Place two couples at each table and instruct them to begin playing the card game at that table. After about eight minutes, blow a whistle, upon which all players lay down their cards and rotate to the next table, picking up in the game where the others left off. Keep rotating on a regular schedule.

Silverware Sculpting

For this game, you need several players who don't know the trick to this game, and at least two people that do. The goal is for those players who don't know the trick to figure it out. One person that knows the trick leaves the room while someone in the group "draws" another person in the group by artistically arranging several pieces of silverware on the table. Everybody left in the room should know who was drawn.

When the person comes back into the room, he looks at the sculpture, studies the arrangement, and then correctly identifies the person who was drawn. The trick is that the other person in the group who knows the trick sits exactly like the person who was drawn. All the guesser has to do is look at her and then look around at the group, see who she is sitting like, and guess that person. This activity can amaze onlookers until they figure out the trick. If somebody in the group thinks he knows the trick, let him have a turn leaving the room while a new sculpture is drawn, and then come back in to identify it.

Slammers And Creepers

Divide your group into two teams. Teams sit opposite each other at a long table. Team #1 has a coin which it secretly passes along to each other underneath the table. At any given time, members of team #2 yell, "Hands!" upon which all members of team #1 must close their fists and raise their clenched hands above their heads. Team #2 then either calls, "Slammers" or "Creepers." If team #2 calls, "Slammers," members of team #1 quickly slam their hands flat onto the table, attempting to conceal the click of the coin. If team #2 calls, "Creepers," members of team #1 carefully place their fists at the edge of the table and slowly spread their fingers out flat, attempting to keep the coin from clicking loudly on the table.

Members of team #2 then attempt to figure out which hand is concealing the coin by discussing where they think it might be and guessing a hand. Team #2 gets a point for each hand left on the table after the coin is found. Switch team roles and play again. Note: If it is too easy to hear the coin as it hits the table, place a tablecloth over the table before playing.

Speed Match

Play this competitive, fast-paced activity with any deck of cards that has matching pairs. Spread the cards out on a table and match them up into pairs. Take one card from each pair and make two identical stacks of cards. To play, spread one of the identical stacks out onto the table face up in random order. Shuffle the remaining stack of cards, form it into a deck, and at the "Go" signal, turn the top card of the deck face up. Participants race to find that card on the table and be the first one to get a hand on it. Whoever touches the card first keeps that match. Play until all of the cards are matched. The player with the most matches wins.

Spoons

Play this fast-handed card game with any deck of cards that provides sets of four. Players sit around a table. Place several spoons in the middle of the table, making sure there is one less spoon than there are players. Deal four cards to each player.

To play, the person left of the dealer picks up a card from the top of the deck and adds it to his hand. He then takes an unwanted card from his hand and passes it face down to the person to his left. This person takes that card and then passes an unwanted card from her hand to the person to her left. The last person places unwanted cards in a discard pile. The goal is to get four cards of a kind in your hand. When someone gets four of a kind, he quickly takes a spoon from the middle of the table. When another player notices that he has taken a spoon, she must also try to grab a spoon. The person who doesn't get a spoon is out of the game. Remove a spoon and play again. Continue playing until only one winner is left.

Variation: Rather than eliminating the player who doesn't get a spoon, give him a point instead. After you're done playing, the person with the lowest score wins.

Toe Painting *Pictionary*

Play this hilarious group date by playing the board game *Pictionary* with the variation that you must draw the pictures with your bare toes on heavy paper after dipping your toes in finger paints. Hang the completed pictures on the wall to dry and to display your creative toe painting art gallery.

Tole Painting

Before this date, get some tole paints, some paintbrushes, a copy of a tole painting pattern for each couple, a basin of water, and a piece of wood cut into the shape of the pattern for each couple. For the date, paint your wood together. You could have a contest to see whose project turns out the prettiest, the craziest, the most unique, or the most like the picture in the pattern book.

White Elephant Christmas Exchange

Each person brings a wrapped white elephant gift (a white elephant gift is a gag gift, usually an unwanted or inexpensive item brought from home) to this date. Everyone sits in a circle facing inward and puts their gifts in the center of the circle. Number several slips of paper beginning with #1, so that there is one numbered slip of paper for each person in attendance. Put the slips of paper in a hat and let each person draw a number.

The person who drew #1 selects a present and unwraps it. She places the gift in front of her so the other people can see it. Then, the person who drew #2 can either take #1's gift, leaving #1 to unwrap a new gift, or he can unwrap his own gift from the center of the circle. The person who drew #3 then can either take #1's or #2's gift or select a wrapped gift from the middle, leaving the person without a gift to open a new gift. The player with the highest number will have the greatest advantage, because he will get to choose whichever gift he wants. Continue playing until all the players have gifts to take home.

Index

Add Up 55
Air Show 55
Airport Welcome Committee . . . 56
Alpine Slide 56
April Fooling 56
Artillery 3
Auction 57
Backwards Track Meet 3
Backword 37
Badminton 4
Balcony Barbecue 92
Balloon Basketball 4
Balloon Bounce 4
Beach Golf 82
Beach Kite Flying 82
Beach Picnic 82
Bicycle Tag 5
Big Game Hunting 5
Big Mouths 92
Birthday Surprise 92
Blindfolded Play Dough
    Sculpting 93
Board Games In A Tent 57
Body Bumping 6
Bopper 6
Breakfast Party 93
British Bulldog 6
Brown Bags 38
Cake Decorating 94
Campfire Stories 57
Candlelight Dinner 57

Candy Making 94
Canning 94
Canoeing 83
Categories 38
Cereal At Sunset 58
Change Challenge 39
Christmas Lights 58
Christmas Tree Decorating 58
Circus 59
Clay Sculpting 95
Climbing Gym 59
Club And Bandanna War 7
Collages And Cookies 95
Cornfield Capture The Flag 59
Crab Soccer 8
Crazy Chain 60
Creative Cookery 95
Croquet 8
Cross Country Skiing 60
Date Drawing 8
"Dear" Hunting 60
Deep Sea Fishing 61
Demolition Derby 62
Digital Photo Shoot 62
Ding-A-Ling Tag 9
Dinner And Olympics 96
Dinner Darts 9
Dinner Hike 62
Dinner On A Train 63
Dinner Theater 63
Display A Date 63

GROUP DATING INDEX

Double-Handed Bowling 63
Down By The Banks 9
Drawing Relay 10
Dress Up Relay 11
Drive-In Restaurant 63
Driving Movie 64
Duck Pond Date 64
Eagle Eyes 39
Easter Egg Color Tag......... 12
Easter Egging 64
Eating Contest 96
Egg Toss 12
Extemporaneous Speaking 40
Fact Or Fiction? 40
Fashion Show Scavenger Hunt ... 65
Fast Blast 13
Fast Food Card Game 65
Fast Food Formal............ 66
Feather Volleyball 13
Feeding Frenzy 13
Feel-N-Name 41
Fine Arts 66
Fireworks 66
Firing Squad................. 83
Fishing 66
Flag Football 14
Flea Market................. 66
Flipper Tennis 67
Float-In Movie 83
Flour Faces.................. 96
Flour War 14
Foreign Dictionary Game 41
Four Wheeling............... 67
Funny Interviews............. 67
Geography 42
German Spotlight............ 15
Glow-Stick Tag............... 15
Guess It..................... 42
Halloween Bowling........... 16

Halloween Ghosting 67
Halloween With The Elderly ... 97
Haunted House 68
Heads-N-Hands 16
Helicopter Ride 68
Hit-N-Run................... 16
Holiday Date 68
Homemade Ice Cream 97
Homemade Water Slide....... 84
Hoop Dodge Ball............. 17
Horse And Buggy Ride 68
Horseback Riding 69
Hospital Visits 69
Hot Air Balloon Ride......... 69
Hot Springs.................. 84
Human Air Hockey 17
Human *Battleship* 84
Human Foosball.............. 18
Human Pinwheel............. 19
Human Tug-O-War 19
Human Tunnel Race 19
Hunter And Hounds 20
Hunter And Hunted.......... 97
Hunting..................... 69
Ice Fishing 70
Ice Skating 70
If/Then 43
Initials..................... 44
International Dinner 97
Jewelry Making 98
Jumping Catch 85
Karaoke 21
Kissing Rugby 21
Kneepad Olympics 21
Laser Tag 70
Laundromat Date............ 70
Lawn Tag 22
Limbo 22
Luck Walk................... 71

Mafia 44	River Rafting 87
Magazine Scavenger Hunt 98	Road Trip 75
Make A Wish 45	Rodeo 75
Mappers 46	Rotating Cards 99
Meals On Wheels 71	S.W.A.T. 75
Mirror Splash 85	Santa Visit 76
Mop Hockey 23	Say What? 49
Mountain Biking 71	Scatter 27
Murder Mystery Party 98	Seventies Date 76
Musical Chairs 23	Shark 87
Name That Tune 46	Signature Scavenger Hunt 76
One Shot 24	Signs 50
Outdoor Movie 71	Silverware Sculpting 99
Paint-Ball 72	Skeet Shooting 77
Party Faces 47	Skits In A Bag 51
Peers On The Pier 87	Slammers And Creepers 100
Person In A Bag 47	Slip-Ball 88
Photograph Scavenger Hunt 72	Smart Formulas 51
Picture Mania 24	Sneaky Sneak 28
Pine Cone Toss 25	Snorkeling 88
Pizza Party 98	Snow Buffalo 28
Planetarium 73	Snow Fort Wars 28
Potato Bowling 25	Snow Volleyball 29
Professions 48	Snowmobiling 77
Progressive Story Writing 99	Snowshoe Olympics 29
Psychiatrist 48	Snowshoe Softball 29
Pumpkin Piñata Party 26	Speed Match 101
Purse And Wallet Scavenger Hunt 26	Spell It 51
Rappelling 73	Spelldown 52
Recipe Book Scavenger Hunt . . . 73	Spoons 101
Red Flag Blue Flag 26	Spray-O-War 88
Red Rover 27	Square Dancing 78
Regressive Dinner 74	Squirts 89
Religious Service 74	State Park 78
Remote Control Car Races 74	Stealth 30
Restaurant Progressive Dinner . . 75	Stretch 30
Ringleader 49	Supercalifragilisticexpialidocious . . . 78
River Picnic 87	Swimming Pool Picnic 90
	Swing Dancing 78

GROUP DATING INDEX

T-Ball 30
Tandem Bike Riding 31
Tap 52
That's Me!. 53
Three-Legged Sports Night 31
Tickle 31
Toe Painting *Pictionary* 102
Toe Races. 31
Tole Painting 102
Tomato War 32
Trampoline Add On 32
Trampoline Catch 32
Trampoline Crack The Egg. 33
Treat Or Tricking. 79
Triangle Game 53
Trivia Scavenger Hunt. 79
Tunnel Ball. 33
Twenty!. 53
Twenty Questions 54
Twister With A Twist 34
Ultimate Frisbee. 34
Unwrap The Present 35
Walleyball. 35
Water Balloon Volleyball. 90
Water Basketball 90
Water Park 90
Water Ring Toss 91
Waterskiing. 91
Weed Salad. 80
Where Are We?. 80
White Elephant Christmas
   Exchange 102
Wolves And Rabbits. 35
Word 54
Yarn Maze Race 36
Your Lucky Date 80
Zoo 80

Other Titles By The Authors:

Dating For Under A Dollar: 301 Ideas

*The Dance Book:
555 Ways to Ask, Answer, and Plan For Dances*

The Book of Mormon Vocabulary Guide

The Doctrine & Covenants Vocabulary Guide

The Triple Combination Vocabulary Guide

Young Men Mutual Activities

Young Women Mutual Activities